Drupal 6 Social Networking

Build a social or community web site with friends lists, groups, custom user profiles, and much more

Michael Peacock

BIRMINGHAM - MUMBAI

Drupal 6 Social Networking

First published: February 2009

Production Reference: 1170209

Published by Packt Publishing Ltd.
32 Lincoln Road
Olton
Birmingham, B27 6PA, UK.

ISBN 978-1-847196-10-1

www.packtpub.com

Cover Image by Vinayak Chittar (vinayak.chittar@gmail.com)

Credits

Author

Michael Peacock

Reviewers

Alan Doucette

Ashok Modi

Dan Kurtz

David Kent Norman

Josh McCormack

Senior Acquisition Editor

Douglas Paterson

Development Editor

Swapna V. Verlekar

Technical Editor

Shadab Khan

Copy Editor

Sumathi Sridhar

Editorial Team Leader

Akshara Aware

Project Manager

Abhijeet Deobhakta

Project Coordinator

Leena Purkait

Indexer

Monica Ajmera

Hemangini Bari

Proofreader

Camille Guy

Production Coordinator

Shantanu Zagade

Cover Work

Shantanu Zagade

About the Author

Michael Peacock (http://www.michaelpeacock.co.uk) is a web developer from Newcastle, UK with a degree in Software Engineering from the University of Durham. After meeting his business partner whilst studying at Durham, he co-founded Peacock Carter (http://www.peacockcarter.co.uk), a Newcastle based creative consultancy specializing in web design, web development, and corporate identity.

Michael loves working on web-related projects, and when he isn't working on client projects he is often tinkering with a web app of his own invention, his latest app is Learnr (http://www.learnr.co.uk).

He has been involved with a number of books, having written three books: *Drupal Social Networks, Selling Online with Drupal e-Commerce, Building Web Stes with TYPO3,* and acted as technical reviewer for *Mobile Web Development* and *Drupal Education & E-Learning.*

You can follow Michael on Twitter: www.twitter.com/michaelpeacock

I'd like to thank everybody at Packt Publishing, in particular: Douglas Paterson for the idea of this book, and for working with me on structuring the book; Leena Purkait for helping to keep the book on track; Swapna Verlekar, the development editor; and Shadab Khan, the technical editor; and of course the technical reviewers, Josh McCormack, David Kent Norman, Ashok Modi, Dan Kurtz, and Alan Doucette, who helped improve the quality of the book.

My thanks also go to my friends and family, in particular my fiancée Emma for her support while working on the book, my Grandfather Neil for continually checking on the progress of my latest book, and my business partner Richard for keeping the business running smoothly during times when I was too busy writing about web sites to make them.

Finally, I'd like to thank you, the reader; I hope that you enjoy this book, and produce a fantasic social networking web site of your own. I look forward to hearing your feedback and seeing what social networking sites you come up with!

About the Reviewers

Ashok Modi is a talented web application programmer who has worked for both large and small tech companies in Toronto and the United States.

Ashok works in Java, PHP, C/ C++/Objective C, SQL and Ruby on Rails. He holds an Honours B.Sc. in computer science from the University of Toronto where he specialized in Software Engineering.

Alan Doucette is a partner of KOI (koitech.net), a web development company. He is passionate about PHP and open source software. He is also very active in the web community and a contributor of Drupal. His constantly changing blog is kept at `http://alanio.net`.

> Thanks go to the awesome Drupal community for all their daily hard work creating great open source software. I would also like to thank my business partner, Ben Davis, for his support and dealing with a Drupal fanatic.

Dan Kurtz is an Internet Strategist and Lead Developer at Trellon LLC, a web development company specializing in open-source social media and content management. Since 2006, he has produced dozens of Drupal sites, helped plan a series of DrupalCamp unconferences, and created the Teleport module for system administrators. When he's not focused on Drupal, he is usually acting in plays or hunched over a sewing machine.

Dan has a BA in Cognitive Science from the University of California, Berkeley and a Master's of Information Studies from University of Toronto. He currently lives in Oakland, California, and maintains an online headquarters at `http://brickswithoutclay.com`.

David Kent Norman has pursued a lifetime of quality education and expertise in technology. His various career pursuits in the past eight years have focused on web-based content management and Drupal. He holds a Bachelor's degree in business, Master's degree in Management Information Systems and a Ph.D. in Instructional Technology.

He published and managed a Content Management System (CMS) with developers from around the world. His CMS was used as the basis for PHP-Nuke and other related projects with more than 8 million downloads. Since he left managing his own CMS project, he has been heavily involved with the Drupal CMS.

Today, David is one of few permanent members of the Drupal Association's General Assembly, a distinction only granted by an election process of peers. In his time with Drupal, David has written or contributed to over 75 modules and themes now freely available for download from Drupal.org. Since 2006, he has been a mentor for the Google Summer of Code program, which brings in new talent to Drupal every year. He was also a reviewer of *Learning Drupal 6*.

Josh McCormack is the owner of InteractiveQA, a social network development company. InteractiveQA uses Drupal to create highly interactive sites that engage visitors to come often, stick around, and generate content. Past and present clients include SonyBMG, Audobon, AsiaSociety.org, Petstyle.com, and others.

Table of Contents

Preface

This book uses Drupal, a powerful and extendable Content Management System (CMS), to set up and manage a social networking web site using a range of powerful and feature-rich social networking modules that are available. By using Drupal, the site can be built and extended rapidly, and changed easily, as the social network evolves and grows.

This book is packed with practical tips not only for setting up a social networking site, but also for promoting and marketing the site, as well as working with the sites' users to help the social network grow and flourish.

What this book covers

Chapter 1 introduces you to Drupal, social networking, and the benefits of creating a social networking site.

Chapter 2 takes you through the Drupal administration interface in addition to discussing how Drupal works. It also walks us through preparing Drupal to become a social networking site.

Chapter 3 goes through the steps of allowing our users to contribute content to the site, using modules which are built into the Drupal core.

Chapter 4 extends the user experience with enhanced customized profiles and blog themes; and enables users to log in using OpenID, which can save them the trouble of remembering another set of login details.

Chapter 5 enables users to interact with one another, as well as build and maintain relationships with each other, forming groups to enhance these relationships and improving site communication and collaboration, and providing areas for users to comment on each other's profiles and viewing the activity of the other users.

Chapter 6 looks at communicating with the users of the social network through mailing lists, theme changes and Twitter feeds, to keep them up-to-date, and improve user retention.

Chapter 7 walks through the creation of a custom module, making use of Google Maps, to illustrate how easily the social network can be extended to meet almost any need. With these skills, the features provided on the social network are no longer limited to the Drupal core and user-contributed modules.

Chapter 8 introduces you to Drupal themes to install and enable new themes, customize existing themes and walks you through the basic steps involved in creating a basic theme of your own, allowing you to provide a unique design to separate your site from the competition.

Chapter 9 shows you how to deploy your new social networking web site, and also how to maintain it to ensure that it is in tip-top condition.

Chapter 10 goes through some useful stages in promoting your site through search engine optimization, social media and advertisements, as well as some useful advice on advertising, promoting, and marketing on the web. This helps to bring back visitors to your site, and also bring in new users.

Appendix A shows you how to install the Apache web server, the PHP interpreter and MySQL database server using the WampServer package.

What you need for this book

Drupal is a free, open source module web application framework and CMS written in PHP that can run in many environments including Windows, Mac OSX, Linux and FreeBSD. All that is required is a development environment set up on your computer such as WAMP, or XAMPP.

To deploy the web site on the Internet, you will need a web hosting account and a domain name. More information on web hosting providers and domain name registrars is provided in Chapter 9.

Who is this book for

This book is for anyone who is interested in creating a social networking web site and would like to make use of Drupal to do so.

This book does not assume you are familiar with Drupal. However, some experience with PHP, HTML and CSS will be useful for some parts of the book, although it is not mandatory.

Conventions

In this book, you will find a number of styles of text that distinguish between different kinds of information. Here are some examples of these styles, and an explanation of their meaning.

Code words in text are shown as follows: "We can include other contexts through the use of the `include` directive."

A block of code will be set as follows:

```
<div class="content clear-block">
 <!-- map -->
    <div id="map" style="width: <?php print $node->width; ?>px;
      height: <?php print $node->height; ?>px"><p>content</p>
    </div>
  <?php print $content ?>
</div>
```

When we wish to draw your attention to a particular part of a code block, the relevant lines or items will be made bold:

```
<div class="content clear-block">
 <!-- map -->
    <div id="map" style="width: <?php print $node->width; ?>px;
      height: <?php print $node->height; ?>px"><p>content</p>
    </div>
  <?php print $content ?>
</div>
```

New terms and **important words** are introduced in a bold-type font. Words that you see on the screen, in menus or dialog boxes for example, appear in our text like this: "The taxonomy options can be accessed from the menu via **Administer | Content management | Taxonomy**".

Warnings or important notes appear in a box like this.

Tips and tricks appear like this.

Reader feedback

Feedback from our readers is always welcome. Let us know what you think about this book, what you liked or may have disliked. Reader feedback is important for us to develop titles that you really get the most out of.

To send us general feedback, simply drop an email to feedback@packtpub.com, making sure to mention the book title in the subject of your message.

If there is a book that you need and would like to see us publish, please send us a note in the **SUGGEST A TITLE** form on www.packtpub.com or email suggest@packtpub.com.

If there is a topic that you have expertise in and you are interested in either writing or contributing to a book, see our author guide on www.packtpub.com/authors.

Customer support

Now that you are the proud owner of a Packt book, we have a number of things to help you to get the most from your purchase.

Downloading the example code for the book

Visit http://www.packtpub.com/files/code/6101_Code.zip to directly download the example code.

The downloadable files contain instructions on how to use them.

Errata

Although we have taken every care to ensure the accuracy of our contents, mistakes do happen. If you find a mistake in one of our books—maybe a mistake in text or code—we would be grateful if you would report this to us. By doing this you can save other readers from frustration, and help to improve subsequent versions of this book. If you find any errata, report them by visiting http://www.packtpub.com/support, selecting your book, clicking on the **let us know** link, and entering the details of your errata. Once your errata are verified, your submission will be accepted and the errata added to the list of existing errata. The existing errata can be viewed by selecting your title from http://www.packtpub.com/support.

Piracy

Piracy of copyright material on the Internet is an ongoing problem across all media. At Packt, we take the protection of our copyright and licenses very seriously. If you come across any illegal copies of our works in any form on the Internet, please provide the location address or web site name immediately so we can pursue a remedy.

Please contact us at `copyright@packtpub.com` with a link to the suspected pirated material.

We appreciate your help in protecting our authors, and our ability to bring you valuable content.

Questions

You can contact us at `questions@packtpub.com` if you are having a problem with some aspect of the book, and we will do our best to address it.

Drupal and Social Networking

1

Welcome to Social Networking with Drupal 6! During the course of this book, we are going to learn how to use **Drupal 6**, a **content management system**, to create a social networking web site. We will install and configure Drupal, take a look at its features and see how it works. By using a combination of existing features, modules, and some simple custom development, we will enable user interaction, user contributions, and communication with our users.

In this chapter, you will learn:

- What social networking is
- About social networking concepts
- What a content management system is
- What Drupal is
- Why Drupal is an excellent platform for social networking
- How to install and configure Drupal

We will also discuss the social networking web site—which we will create during the course of this book—*DinoSpace! a social network for keepers of pet dinosaurs.*

Social networking

Social networking and social network services seem to be taking the Internet by storm, moving from large services such as Facebook and MySpace to simpler services such as Twitter and FriendFeed. But what exactly is social networking and what does a social networking service (like the one we will create in this book) do?

One of the fundamental concepts of social networking is building connections with other people. These connections and their connections build up a network of social links between users. With a network of contacts, it becomes easier to contact new people, perhaps someone who is a friend of a friend, or contact people you have lost touch with, such as old classmates. Obviously, using a social network to reconnect with people who you know or have known physically would require either a large social network (such as Facebook or MySpace) or a niche social network such as our DinoSpace scenario (why not reconnect with people you met at a recent dinosaur care conference?).

Let's take a look at how these networks of contacts are built up.

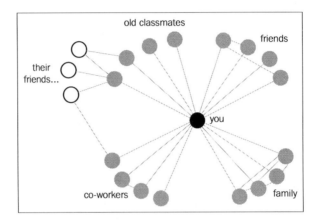

The network representation above shows the connections between contacts. Contacts of a contact can be easily discovered, making it easy to build up your own contacts to communicate and collaborate with new people.

There is another side to social networks, and that is the community, contribution and collaboration aspect. Social networking sites generally allow interaction between users in a way that expands the social networking site itself, by contributing to the content of the site, communicating via discussion forums and blogs, making the site grow organically and become the product of all its contributors. Let's look at the collaborative and communicative features available on most social networks:

- Discussions, normally by means of a discussion forum
- Photograph galleries, allowing images to be shared with contacts, and in some cases associated with the people in them
- Custom profiles that allow users to share information about themselves with others
- Personal messaging and personal contact forms that allow users to communicate with each other directly

Many social networks also have the ability to work with information from other web sites and services, allowing you to bring together your information from other sites (such as tweets from your Twitter feed, photos from your Flickr stream, links from your `del.icio.us` profile, and so on), and to help find friends already on the web site using contacts from your email address book.

These features are just the tip of the iceberg. If you are already familiar with social networking services such as Facebook and MySpace, then you will know that they provide a wealth of features and services for their users. If you are not familiar, why not sign up to a few services and have a look at what they offer; it might help you while planning for your own social network. There are also some less popular social-networking-type sites such as Twitter (`www.twitter.com`) and FriendFeed (`www.friendfeed.com`) which particularly work well with building friendships between people who don't actually know each other, whereas Facebook and MySpace are designed with "real life" friends in mind.

Why create a social network instead of joining an existing one?

There are already a number of popular and powerful social networks available, as I've mentioned above, so why would we want to create our own social network?

- Improve business—A social network can allow businesses to interact informally with customers, gathering feedback and in some cases giving value to the customer. One particular instance of this is that of radio stations advertising their web sites as social-network-type web sites, where listeners can get in touch, connect with other listeners, request songs, share photographs, and so on.

- Improve communications—Communicate with users informally, easily and cheaply.

- Provide a service—With the site we are going to create throughout this book, we will be providing a service through the exchange of knowledge and information relating to owning pet dinosaurs and having our own social network provide a fantastic platform for sharing and expanding this knowledge.

- They are fun! Social networks break down the barriers of time and distance, and are a good way to meet new people in a relatively safe way.

Let's look into some of the reasons I've just listed which will answer why we should create our own social network, as opposed to using an existing one.

Improve business

Existing social networks do allow us to improve business, because we can tap into their existing user base, which is great; but where it falls short is in providing extra enhancements. If we look at Facebook, additional features are created by third-party developers, and embedded as applications. Some of these applications add business functionality, for instance the one that allows users to make reservations for a local restaurant. The problem with such applications is that users are prompted for permission before the application gets any of their information (rightly so, as they are hosted by the developers who write them, and are different from Facebook). With the rise in the number of available applications, and the amount of "invitation spam" inviting users to add applications, many users are more careful and reserved when it comes to using applications within Facebook. With our own social network, we wouldn't need to worry about this. We would host all the information, and can provide exactly what we need—a streamlined social network (without adding extra features, bloating the web site).

Enable communication

Social networks are designed to enable and enhance communication. We have no physical barriers to communication (as being in a country different from another user isn't relevant). So, both an existing social network, and our own would improve communications. The advantage of having our own site is that we are less restricted in how we can communicate with our users. We can easily contact them and display information to them via any area of the web site, email, personal messaging and possibly via mobile devices too.

Provide a service

Many web sites and social networks provide services relevant to the social network, or to the target audience, such as linking with Amazon to show books a user has read, or a knowledge base of information.

Services provided through other social networks, either via standard functionality they offer, or via third-party plug-ins (such as Facebook applications) would be restricted in a number of ways—firstly, by the terms and conditions of the social network, and later by how additional functionalities can be added. For instance, if we were to create a knowledge base for taking care of pet dinosaurs as an application in a social network, it relies on being promoted within the social network's web site (as it is difficult enough to try and promote a web site to new visitors, let alone a particular part of a web site). Its functionality and design is also limited to the provisions made by that social network for third-party plug-ins.

So why create a social network?

It really comes down to the nature of what you want to offer the end users. If you want a social network to fill a particular niche, then creating one is probably the best bet. If you want to create a generic social network or a specific social networking feature for a generic audience, then utilizing an existing social network would be more productive, as you could harness their system and their user base.

DinoSpace!

Throughout this book, we are going to create our very own social networking web site using Drupal. This web site is called DinoSpace!, and it is aimed at the owners of pet dinosaurs (yes, I know, nobody really owns a pet dinosaur…it would be too expensive and impractical) to interact with one another. In particular, the web site aims to:

- Connect owners of pet dinosaurs and allow them to build and maintain friendships with other users
- Allow owners to share stories about their pets
- Help in promoting dinosaur-friendly places to visit
- Provide interactive help and support to fellow dinosaur owners
- Allow owners to chart their activities with their dinosaur

Of course, the web site needs to enable more than just user-to-user interactions. It also needs to provide other content, and allow communication between us, the managers of the web site, and our users to keep them up-to-date.

We are going to create our own social networking web site. To do that, we are going to use Drupal, an open-source content management system (CMS). So, let's look at exactly what a CMS is, and what Drupal is.

What is a CMS?

Before we look into exactly what a CMS is, let us look at the problem with web sites, which leads to the need for content management solutions.

Most web sites available on the Internet involve a degree of complexity, be it large web sites with a lot of content, or those dealing with dynamic user interactions, or those involving a number of different people updating different sections. Even small web sites can be complicated to manage, particularly if the design needs a change, or a particular piece of information needs a change on every page.

One of the key features of a content management system is that it separates the design of a web site, the content of a web site and its business logic and features, making it easy to change any aspect of the web site independently without affecting the rest of the web site.

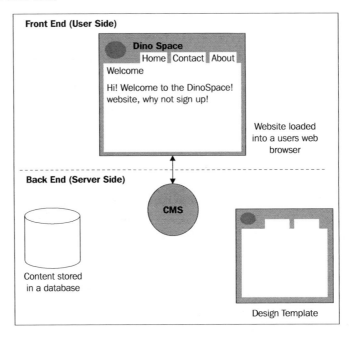

The diagram above shows the separation of these key layers. It shows that when a visitor to the web site requests a page, the content management system takes the design template and the content from the database, combines the two along with some logic (such as seeing if the visitor is logged in, in which case it may display a username too) and then sends the result to the visitor's web browser.

Generally, content management systems have the ability for users to do the following through their web browser:

- Create content
- Edit, delete and manage content
- Provide and restrict access to content, and to enable editing of content by the user's role within the web site

- Allow multiple users to easily edit and control different areas of a web site simultaneously
- Separate the design, content, and logic layers of the web site
- Collaborate effectively
- Manage different versions or drafts of content (referred to as revisions in Drupal)

What is Drupal?

Drupal is a free, open source content management system which allows individuals, or a community of users to easily publish, manage, and organize a wide variety of content on a web site.

The project was started by Dries Buytaert, and is now assisted in development with a large community. One particular advantage with Drupal is its modular framework, which allows additional features to be plugged into it, in the form of modules. The Drupal web site maintains an extensive list of modules and themes (custom designs), which can be used for free.

The Drupal web site address is www.drupal.org, and it contains the downloads, news and updates on Drupal, information relating to many of the modules, and themes which can be downloaded to enhance Drupal and discussion forums.

Drupal as a social networking platform

Because of the way Drupal is structured, it is very flexible in adapting to the needs of a wide range of different web sites. Permission to perform various actions such as creating content, writing a comment, writing a blog post and so on can all be assigned to different roles within Drupal, be it the role of an administrative user or the role of a standard user who is logged in. This means we can grant the permissions to contribute and help in managing the content of the web site to the users of the web site.

Many socially-oriented features are included in Drupal "out of the box" (without the need to download extra files or modules) including:

- Blogs
- Forums
- Contact forms
- Collaborative content via the book module and also via permissions allowing users to edit different types of content, such as pages

Drupal's modular framework, which I mentioned earlier, allows new features to be installed at a later time. There are many modules available, which are designed to enhance Drupal's ability to work and act like a social network. It also means that once our site is up and running, we can easily expand it at a later date with new modules to add extra functionality. Such modules include:

- Organic groups
- Extended profiles
- Blog themes
- Gravitar
- OpenID

With Drupal being a content management system, we also have the advantage of having our site controlled and managed by ourselves, as is typical of most web sites, while the community can contribute to the other areas.

Installing Drupal

We know what Drupal is, we know what social networking is, and we know what we are going to create during the course of this book. So, let's get started! The first thing we need to do is install Drupal. This section contains some detailed technical information regarding the requirements and installation of Drupal.

For most of the book, we will be working with Drupal installed locally on our own computers (see *Appendix*, for setting up a development environment if you don't have web server software installed on your own computer) as we build up our site. We will move it across to a live web site later.

Requirements

If you already have a development environment set up, which differs from the one detailed in *Appendix*, then you may need to make some adjustments to take into account the server requirements for Drupal. If you went through the process in *Appendix*, you will find that everything is set up and ready, and compatible with Drupal.

- Web server (Apache recommended, and used during the course of the book; IIS is also supported. However, other web servers have had limited testing)
- PHP 4.3.5 or greater (5.2 or higher recommended; this will be the minimum requirement once Drupal 7 is released)

- Database Engine: Either MySQL (4.1 or 5) or PostgreSQL (7.4 or greater). MySQL is assumed during the course of this book.

- To make use of friendly or clean URLs, `mod_rewrite` and the ability to use `.htaccess` files is required. However, it is optional.

- PHP's XML extension may be required to utilize certain XML-based services. This is also optional.

The Drupal handbook contains more details on the requirements, `http://drupal.org/requirements`. There are also some guidelines on setting up your own development server environment on the Drupal web site at `http://drupal.org/node/260`. However, in this book we are assuming the setup given in *Appendix*.

Download

We can download a copy of Drupal from the download page on the Drupal web site `http://drupal.org/download`. There are a number of download areas on the Drupal web site. But this one is specifically for the Drupal project (that is, the content management system itself), which is exactly what we want. The version we want to download is one from the 6.x range (at the time of writing, 6.5). So let's click the download link and download Drupal!

Installation

Now that we have downloaded a copy of Drupal 6, we need to install it onto our local web server. To do that we need to:

- Extract the Drupal files
- Create a database
- Run the Drupal installer

The file we have downloaded is a compressed file containing all the individual files that make up Drupal. We need to extract this into the web folder in our development environment (see *Appendix*) using an unzipping program (such as WinZip, PowerArchiver or Windows' built-in "Compressed folders" system, or the default program for handling compressed files on your computer).

Technical Installation Details

There are more technical installation details available in the `INSTALL.txt` file, which is in the folder we have just extracted.

We need a database for Drupal to store information such as the web site's content, details of our users, settings, and so on. PHPMyAdmin is a web-based tool for administering MySQL databases. Most web hosts provide access to it, and we have a copy on our local machine too.

Let's log in to phpMyAdmin and create our database. Our local installation is located at `http://localhost/phpmyadmin/`. We will need to have our database username and password to hand (see Appendix A, if you are using that development environment). Most of the development environment software such as WAMP, XAMPP, and so on have a default username of `root` without a password.

Once logged in there, we have the option to create a new database. Let's call it `Drupal`.

 Keep a note of the database name, as well as the database username and password, as we will need it in a minute when we run the Drupal installer.

Now that we have our database, we can run the installer. To do that, we just need to visit the folder where we installed Drupal, using our web browser. This should be at `http://localhost/drupal-6.2/`. Since we haven't installed Drupal yet, visiting this page will take us straight to the installer, which initially asks us which language we would like to install it in.

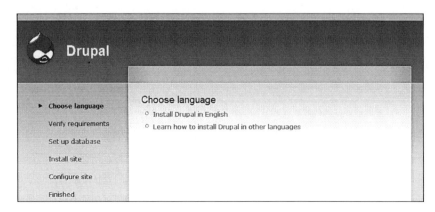

After clicking **Install Drupal in English**, we are taken to the Database configuration options.

We now need to enter the **Database name**, **Database username** and our **Database password**. This information is necessary, so Drupal can connect to the database and install the default data.

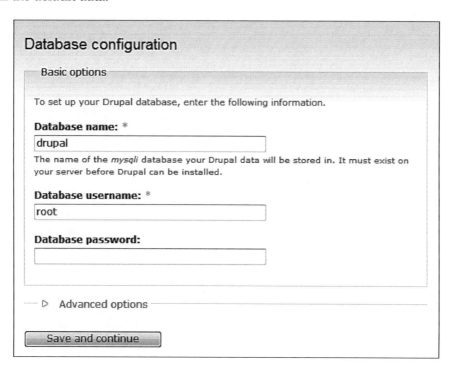

We shouldn't need the **advanced options**. However, there may be times when we'd need it for some shared hosting providers. It allows us to set the server on which the database is stored (for us, it is our local machine, which is localhost; this is the value which is already set), the port the database uses (which can normally be left blank) and a prefix for the database. If you want to have more than one installation of Drupal from the same database, you need to enter a unique prefix for each of the installations. For our local installation, we don't need to worry about them. So let's click **Save and continue**.

The installer then sets up the database, which would take a couple of minutes.

Now that the database is set up, we need to provide some basic site information, the details for our administrator user account and a few server settings.

The basic site information we need to provide is the name of the web site and the email address to be used by the web site when sending emails.

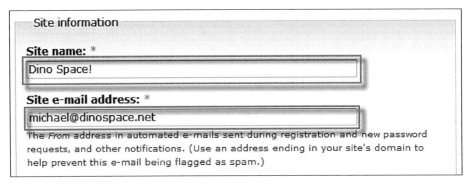

Since our site is going to be called **Dino Space!** Let's enter it in the **Site name** field, and an appropriate email address in the **Site e-mail address** field.

The next section is for the details of our **administrative user account**. This user account will have permissions to manage and control the entire site. To create the account, we need to supply a **Username**, an **E-mail address**, and a **Password** (which needs to be confirmed).

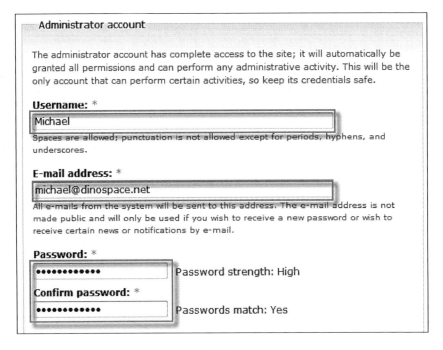

I've entered **Michael** for the **Username** and my email address of **michael@dinospace.net** for the **E-mail address**, followed by my **Password**. You should enter a **Username**, **E-mail address** and **Password** of your choice.

Drupal analyzes the **Password** you type in to check its security and suitability for use. Because this **Administrator account** can control the entire site, having an insecure password can leave the site vulnerable to the **Administrator account** being hacked into. If you enter a **Password** which Drupal thinks is too insecure, it gives you some tips (as shown in the following screenshot) to make your **Password** more secure.

The password does not include enough variation to be secure. Try:

○ Adding both upper and lowercase letters.

○ Adding punctuation.

Here are some guidelines I generally follow when creating passwords which I feel is worth pointing out:

- Use at least eight characters
- Use letters and numbers—personally I like to use certain numbers as letters, for example, m1ch4el
- Use upper- and lowercase letters
- Add punctuation, for example, M1ch@eL
- If I'm using a word, I'd like to spell it incorrectly, for example, M1kh@3IL

Finally, we have the server settings options. The only options required are the **Default time zone**, **Clean URLs** and **Update notifications** options. The **Default time zone** option is to determine the dates and times used throughout the site. So if we were to post an article on the web site, it would use the time zone set here when displaying the date and time the article was posted. The **Clean URLs** option makes the URLs generated by Drupal more user-friendly, and more search-engine, friendly too. This setting depends on the servers' setup. Some web servers cannot support clean URLs because of the way the pages are generated. However, Drupal does a quick test to see if our server supports them. The final option, if set, will notify us about the new versions of Drupal when they are available.

This is very useful, particularly from a security perspective, where some vulnerability in security may have been reported and fixed in a newer version. This will alert us to the availability of this version.

Server settings

Default time zone:

Thursday, May 22, 2008 - 15:14 +0100 ▾

By default, dates in this site will be displayed in the chosen time zone.

Clean URLs:

⊙ Disabled

◉ Enabled

This option makes Drupal emit "clean" URLs (i.e. without ?q= in the URL).

Your server has been successfully tested to support this feature.

Update notifications:

☑ Check for updates automatically

With this option enabled, Drupal will notify you when new releases are available. This will significantly enhance your site's security and is **highly recommended**. This requires your site to periodically send anonymous information on its installed components to drupal.org. For more information please see the update notification information.

The default time zone picked up should be the one set on our computer, and shouldn't need to be changed. We can enable **Clean URLs**, assuming our server supports them, and we should check the updates checkbox.

Time zone and Clean URLs

If you are installing Drupal direct onto a web hosting server, the time zone will be that of the server, which if located in some other country, may need to be set to match the time zone you prefer. **Clean URL** support may not be available; you should contact your web host if you are unsure about it or you need support.

Once we are done, we need to click the **Save and continue** button to complete the Drupal installation!

We are now presented with a confirmation screen informing us that the Drupal installation is complete. You might have a few errors on this page relating to Drupal's ability to send email.

> ## Drupal installation complete
>
> * warning: mail() [function.mail]: Failed to connect to mailserver at "localhost" port 25, verify your "SMTP" and "smtp_port" setting in php.ini or use ini_set () in C:\wamp\www\drupal-6.2\includes\mail.inc on line 193.
> * Unable to send e-mail. Please contact the site admin, if the problem persists.
>
> Congratulations, Drupal has been successfully installed.
>
> Please review the messages above before continuing on to your new site.

This error message is expected, because we have installed Drupal on our local computer, and our computer probably does not have a built-in email server (although if you are running a Linux computer or a Mac, you may have one built-in, depending on your setup). This isn't something we need to worry about, as we won't need it to send emails until we deploy our web site live on the web!

Clicking the **your new site** link takes us to our brand new Drupal installation.

Configuring Drupal

Since we have just set up Drupal, and created our user account, we are now logged into our new web site. On this front page, we have a link to the configuration section where we can configure our installation.

1. **Configure your website**

   Once logged in, visit the administration section, where you can customize and configure all aspects of your website.

The **customize and configure** link takes us to the **Site Configuration** page, which contains various sections of the options we can configure.

Site configuration

Actions
Manage the actions defined for your site.

Administration theme
Settings for how your administrative pages should look.

Clean URLs
Enable or disable clean URLs for your site.

Date and time
Settings for how Drupal displays date and time, as well as the system's default timezone.

Error reporting
Control how Drupal deals with errors including 403/404 errors as well as PHP error reporting.

File system
Tell Drupal where to store uploaded files and how they are accessed.

Image toolkit
Choose which image toolkit to use if you have installed optional toolkits.

Input formats
Configure how content input by users is filtered, including allowed HTML tags. Also allows enabling of module-provided filters.

Logging and alerts
Settings for logging and alerts modules. Various modules can route Drupal's system events to different destination, such as syslog, database, email, ...etc.

Performance
Enable or disable page caching for anonymous users and set CSS and JS bandwidth optimization options.

Site information
Change basic site information, such as the site name, slogan, e-mail address, mission, front page and more.

Site maintenance
Take the site off-line for maintenance or bring it back online.

Let us take a look at these options and what they allow us to do, and configure them for our DinoSpace site.

Actions

Actions are tasks which Drupal can perform, such as unpublishing a comment, making a post sticky, or sending an email. These actions can be performed by some of the modules within Drupal when triggered by a certain event. For instance, we could automatically set posts or comments containing links to the competing web sites to be unpublished.

On their own, these actions won't do anything, they need to be triggered. However, triggers are not enabled by default, different modules and custom development may introduce the need for actions and triggers later.

Administration theme

The **Administration theme** setting allows us to set a different theme when on the administration pages.

 A **Theme** is a collection of files, which make up the design, layout, and style of our Drupal web site. New themes can be added, modified, and applied to change the look of our site. In Chapter 8, *Designing our Site*, we will look at themes in detail.

Since we don't know what these different themes look like, we can't yet make a judgement on whether we would prefer a different one for administering the site. The advantage of this is that if we were to have a very stylish image-heavy design for our site, we may opt for a simpler design for the administration options to make it easier and faster to administer the site, while keeping the site itself more visually appealing. There is also the option to use the **Administration theme** when editing and creating content, which is generally done outside the **Administration section**.

Clean URLs

We have already set the **Clean URLs** option, when we installed Drupal. But this section allows us to change this, and enable or disable the **Clean URLs** at any time, should we need to. We don't need to; so, let's leave this as it is.

 What is a clean URL?
Without this option enabled, URLs in Drupal will look like this:
`www.dinospace.net/?=node/83`; whereas with the option enabled, it will look like this: `www.dinospace.net/node/83`.

Date and time

The **Date and time** settings allow us to change the locale and format of the date and time used, including:

- The default time zone (which we set on installation).
- User-configurable time zones (to allow users to set their own time zones, which adjust the display of dates for them). This is already enabled, and makes a more enjoyable experience for users in another time zone, as it may be difficult for users to find out what time something was posted or replied to.
- The first day of the week, used for calendar views.
- Format of the short representation of a date.
- Format of a medium length representation of a date.
- Format of a long length representation of a date.

The formatting settings are primarily a personal choice, I'm happy with them as they are, so I'm going to leave them at their defaults. Why don't you explore these options and adjust them to your personal taste.

Error reporting

Using the **Error reporting** settings, we can specify a page to redirect the user to if they try to access a page which either they have no permission to view, or which does not exist.

We haven't actually created any pages yet. So we can't redirect our users. However, we will come back to this in Chapter 2, *Preparing Drupal for a Social Networking Site*.

The other option on the page is with regards to displaying technical error messages generated by Drupal. The two options available are **Write errors to the log and to the screen** and **Write errors to the log**. These error messages are useful when developing and creating a site. However, displaying them to visitors can confuse them, as they will be technical, and can pose a security risk by revealing information on our site's setup. Let's change this **to Write errors to the log**. If we do encounter any problems, we can always check the log.

If you wish to leave it as it is, don't forget to change it to just the log when you put your site live on the web!

Error reporting:

Write errors to the log ▾

Specify where Drupal, PHP and SQL errors are logged. While it is recommended that a site running in a production environment write errors to the log only, in a development or testing environment it may be helpful to write errors both to the log and to the screen.

Save configuration   Reset to defaults

Once we have made those changes, we can click on the **Save configuration** button, and then return to the configuration options by clicking the **Site configuration** link near the top of the page.

File system

The **File system** options determine where the files that we may allow our users to upload to our site or download from our site are stored. There are settings for:

- **File system path** — this is the location on the server where the files will be stored.

- **Temporary directory** — where uploaded files are stored during previews.

- **Download method** (either **public** or **private**) — **Public downloads** mean that anyone could gain access to the files as they are stored in a web accessible folder, whereas the private method would require Drupal to generate the download for the user. The **Private method** is useful, if we don't want guests to be able to download the files and only want registered users to access them.

Changing the download method on a site which is in use can cause problems with the existing files. So now is the perfect time to change this if we need to. For DinoSpace, there is no reason to have the files tagged private, so let's leave these options as they are.

Changing the download method, and a note on the temporary path

If you do change the download method, you should change the file system path to reflect a location which isn't accessible via the Internet, that is, outside your web site's root directory. The temporary path is generated automatically based on your server's settings; change this only if you know what you are doing. When working on a live web site in a hosting environment, your web host should be able to instruct how you should configure the file system path and the temporary directory settings, should you wish to change them, or use the private download method.

Image toolkit

Many web servers provide options for manipulating images, the most common ones are the GD image library and ImageMagick. We have the GD library installed (from Appendix A). However, we could remove this, or use the ImageMagick library instead. These libraries provide options for tasks including things like:

- Adding watermarks
- Changing the size of an image
- Cropping an image
- Converting the format of images
- Combining images

The **Image toolkit** settings provide settings specific to the image library (or toolkit as Drupal refers to it) we have installed. With the GD library, the only setting is related to the quality of images which are manipulated by Drupal.

By default, this is 75%, which means if we were to upload an image and we set Drupal to generate a thumbnail, the thumbnail image would only be 75% of the quality it could be. This option weighs the quality of the image over the size of the image. If we increase the quality of the images, uploaded images will be of a larger size, which may take longer to download, whereas if we reduce the quality of the image, we get lower file sizes, however, the quality of the images is reduced.

Let's adjust this to **85%**, as we want to use high-quality images on our site. If this becomes a problem, we can always change it later. You may find it useful to adjust this setting letter if the additional bandwidth is not an issue for you, or the quality of the image is too poor.

Then we need to click **Save configuration** and return to the **Site configuration** page.

Input formats

 Please note that this section is a little more advanced than the other settings pages, as it requires a little more technical understanding.

The **Input formats** dictate how Drupal should process data which a user has supplied, and depending on the user, we may wish to assign a different format.

The two formats available are:

- Filtered HTML
- Full HTML

Filtered HTML only allows certain HTML tags, and automatically converts web addresses into links, and new lines into paragraphs where appropriate (although this can be altered). The **Full HTML** option allows all HTML tags, including things such as JavaScript which could potentially be harmful, if they were submitted by a malicious user. You should never offer this input format to people outside your circle of trust. This would be a serious security risk and should only be available to those who are trusted and involved in the creation of your web site, not general users of the site.

 HTML tags are used to structure a web site, for instance, a paragraph would be contained within <p> and </p> tags, and a hyperlink would be contained within the <a> </a> tags. Different tags do different things and pose different risks.

The roles column in the table of **Input formats** indicate which users can use which format. By default, only administrators can use full HTML (although it says no roles may use it, anyone who can administer the input formats can also use them all). Let's look at the configuration options for **Filtered HTML**, which will be the input format our users will use, and see what we can configure. The **configure** link allows us to configure the input format.

Default	Name	Roles	Operations	
◉	Filtered HTML	All roles may use default format	configure	
○	Full HTML	No roles may use this format	configure	delete

Users are grouped into roles; by default, there are anonymous user roles (users who are not logged in) and authenticated user roles. The roles define the permissions for those users. However, the administrator user created when installing Drupal has permission to do anything on the site.

Configurable options include the roles which can use the format, and the filters which the format has. We can't adjust the roles, because this is the default format. So all roles must be enabled for this format.

Currently, any web addresses entered by our visitors will be turned into a hyperlink to that site. Unchecking this may help prevent spam. However the <a> tag is still allowed, so links could still be created.

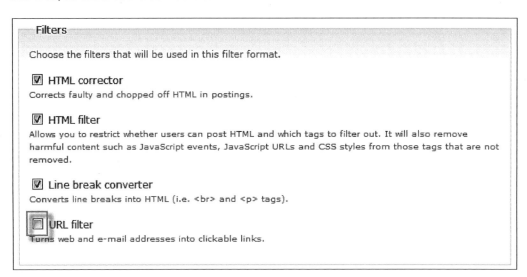

Instead, let's enable the spam link deterrent option. This option is found by clicking the **Configure** link at the top of the page, which also allows us to edit the specific HTML tags that are not allowed by this input format.

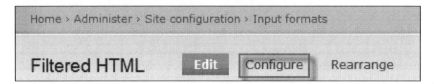

These configuration options allow us to set:

- The maximum length of text in a link (longer links will be shortened)
- How tags should be filtered
- Tags that are allowed
- Whether help on HTML should be shown

The **Spam link deterrent** option adds a special bit of code to all the links that are submitted, which tell the search engines that we don't have editorial control over the content. This prevents the search engine from penalizing our search engine rankings if that link turns out to be a spam link.

☑ Spam link deterrent

If enabled, Drupal will add rel="nofollow" to all links, as a measure to reduce the effectiveness of spam links. Note: this will also prevent valid links from being followed by search engines, therefore it is likely most effective when enabled for anonymous users.

Let's enable this option by checking the box, and then click the **Save configuration** button to save the change.

Logging and alerts

The next setting is for Logs and alerts, which currently only contains options for database logging. This sets how many logs should be retained, and by default, is set to keep the last 1000 log entries. These logs are viewable from the administration area. For the cut-off limit to work, we need to set up a scheduled task, called a Cron job, which we will look at in Chapter 9, *Deploying and Maintaining our Site*. Until then, changing this option won't do anything. So, let's leave it for now.

Logs include actions such as creating content, updating content and performing administration tasks. It is important to keep some of these, as it may help in keeping tabs on other administrators, or in investigating why a user had a problem doing something with the site. But the system stores logs for lots of different things, and it can soon build up and clog the database; so we don't want to keep too many of these for too long!

Performance

Next, we have **Performance settings**. These settings allow us to optimize the performance of our Drupal installation, which is particularly useful when we have lots of visitors to our web site. The **Normal** caching mode is recommended for production sites, but we are still working on our site. So we will need to remember to change this when we deploy our site.

Page caching prevents Drupal from loading and processing pages every time they are requested. Instead, it stores a copy of the processed page (known as a cached version) and when anonymous users visit the site (who are less likely to use dynamic elements that require processing, Drupal serves them the cached version of the page. With web sites under a lot of strain, caching is very useful in reducing unnecessary load on the server from many visits. The **Minimum cache lifetime** setting prevents Drupal from processing the page too frequently. This ensures that the cached version is used for at least a specific time period, before a new, more up-to-date copy is processed, and the cached version is updated. This setting is more suited for very busy sites.

Every time a user visits our site, data is transferred from our web server (well it will be when we have it deployed; for now, it is stored on our local computer, and is not being transferred) to the user. This data transfer is usually within a specific bandwidth limit set by hosting companies or service providers. Very busy sites can use lots of bandwidth, which can in turn cost the web site owners a lot of money. Drupal has some basic **Bandwidth optimizations** available for us to reduce the amount of data transferred.

Bandwidth optimizations

Drupal can automatically optimize external resources like CSS and JavaScript, which can reduce both the size and number of requests made to your website. CSS files can be aggregated and compressed into a single file, while JavaScript files are aggregated (but not compressed). These optional optimizations may reduce server load, bandwidth requirements, and page loading times.

These options are disabled if you have not set up your files directory, or if your download method is set to private.

Optimize CSS files:

⦿ Disabled

⦾ Enabled

This option can interfere with theme development and should only be enabled in a production environment.

Optimize JavaScript files:

⦿ Disabled

⦾ Enabled

This option can interfere with module development and should only be enabled in a production environment.

We are not anticipating a large number of users to our social network, at least, not right away; so let's leave those **Disabled** for now. We can always keep an eye on our bandwidth usage and enable it later if we need to.

Site information

The **Site information** options give us a few options which we can actually alter now, as they relate to what the site is, and what it is for. The options available are:

- **Site name**—The name of the site, which in our case is **Dino Space!** This was set when we installed Drupal
- **Site e-mail address**—The email address from which automated emails from the web site will be sent; this was also set at the time of installation
- **Slogan**—A motto or tag line for the site
- **Mission**—A mission or focus statement
- **Footer message**—A message to be displayed at the bottom of each page, in the footer
- The names of anonymous users
- The page which will act as our front page

We already have our name and email address set at the time of Drupal installation; so let's set the other options.

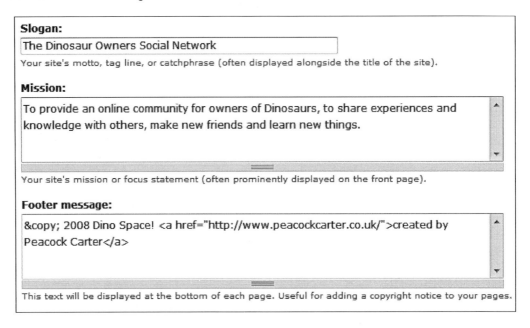

Out of the remaining options, we already have a name for the anonymous users, and as we have not created any pages, we can't set our default front page just yet!

Site maintenance

The final configuration option is the **Site maintenance** settings. This allows us to take our web site offline, so that only administrators can access it and display a message to visitors trying to get in. This would be useful when making big changes, which could interfere with what our visitors are doing on the site at that time. So during these updates, we would take the site offline to prevent any problems.

When we put our web site online, we will need to tweak some settings before they become usable. So, let's set a message now saying something along the lines of the site currently being configured for use. That way, when we put the site online, we can put it into maintenance mode, and it will display the message we have set now.

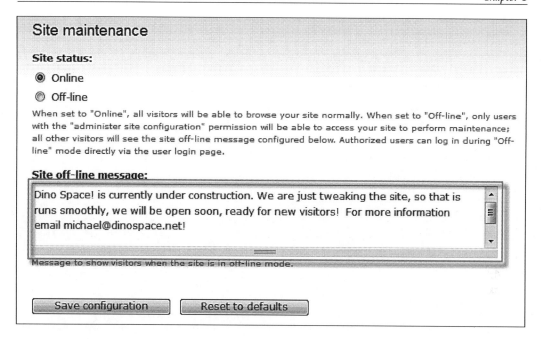

We have now done as much configuration as possible at this stage!

Logged out when in maintenance mode?
You can always log back in from the
`http://localhost/Drupal-6.2/user/login` page.

Summary

We have looked into what social networking is and at various social networking concepts, and also seen why we may wish to create a social network. We then looked at Drupal, and have now become aware of what it is, and how it can be used as a social networking platform. Finally, we installed Drupal onto our local development environment, examined the configuration options available and made some basic configuration changes to the default Drupal installation.

The next stage is to start preparing our site to become a social network!

2
Preparing Drupal for a Social Networking Site

Now that we have looked into social networking, how we can use Drupal as a social networking platform and we have installed Drupal, we need to start preparing our Drupal installation for use as a social networking site!

In this chapter, you will learn:

- How Drupal works
- How to use Drupal
- How to use the administration tools within Drupal
- About taxonomy and RSS within Drupal
- More about planning your site and its content

How Drupal works

Before we start building our social networking site, it is important to take a step back and look at Drupal a bit more in detail, to see how it works and the thought process behind it. Having a better understanding of this will help when planning, expanding, and managing our site!

An abstract framework

Although in the previous chapter, I described Drupal as a content management system, it can more accurately be described as a content management framework. While it is still a content management system, that is, it is a system used for managing content within a web site, Drupal places more emphasis on easy customization and configuration.

Drupal is an abstract framework, because instead of focusing on specific solutions and situations, it focuses more on generic problems and their solutions, which makes it useful in many situations. Further, with a little customization, it can be tailor-made to provide specific solutions.

Nodes

Nodes are what make Drupal an **abstract** framework. Most content types within Drupal are variants of a central concept within Drupal—the node. While different types of node (that is, different **Content Types**) are managed and handled differently, they are all stored together in the database. The Drupal web site explains this best on their general concepts page:

The main building block of Drupal is a node. The word 'node' does not suggest that it is a part of some network. On the contrary, you should think of a node as a single puzzle piece that is placed onto the site by one of your users, or even yourself. A node can be part of a forum, a blog or a book, and by using the Content Construction Kit, you can create as many custom node types as you want. Remember that each node has a type, referred to as a Content Type. It also has a Node ID, a Title, a Body, a creation date, an author and some other properties. It is stored together with all other nodes in one big "shoe-box" known as a "table" in your database.

For more information on this go to http://drupal.org/node/19828 *Drupal— General Concepts*

 The Content Construction Kit mentioned above, is a third party module, and is not available out of the box.

Although Drupal only has Story and Page nodes available when it is first installed, the optional core modules that comes included with it, have provisions for the following nodes:

- Blog entries
- Pages of a collaborative book (similar to a Wiki)
- Comments (although these are not nodes) which allow users to comment on nodes
- Forum
- Page
- Poll
- Story

Nodes and content types are sometimes used interchangeably in this book.

Content flags

When managing the content (which we will look at shortly), we can set various "flags" or statuses on the content including:

- Published—indicates that the content is visible to site visitors.
- Unpublished—indicates that the content is not visible to site visitors.
- Promoted—indicates that the content has been promoted to the front page of the site.
- Not promoted—indicates that the content has not been promoted to the front page of the site.
- Sticky—indicates whether the content has been marked "sticky". Sticky content is displayed above non-sticky content, even if some new content has been posted to the site.
- Not sticky—indicates that the content has not been marked as "sticky".

Let's take a brief look at exactly what they mean, so that we understand these concepts when we come to use them later.

Published and unpublished content

Obviously, this isn't something that can be illustrated via a screenshot; the content is either visible to our users or not visible to our users. Of course, users with permissions to see the unpublished content will be able to see it!

Promoted and not promoted content

If content has been promoted to the front page, then it will appear on the front page of our Drupal site. The following image illustrated pages that have been created for the news items promoted to the front page.

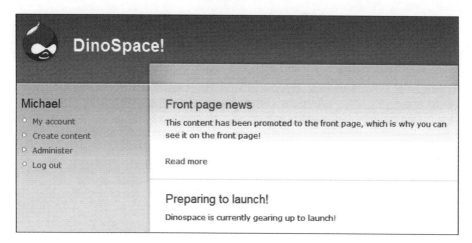

Content that hasn't been promoted to the front page obviously isn't displayed there. The content is split into a summary, which is shown on the front page. The rest of the content is read by clicking the **read more** link associated with the content.

Sticky and not sticky content

Content which is sticky appears above other posted items at the top of a page, for instance, we have some sticky content which has been promoted to the front page, and beneath it is some newer content that was not made sticky.

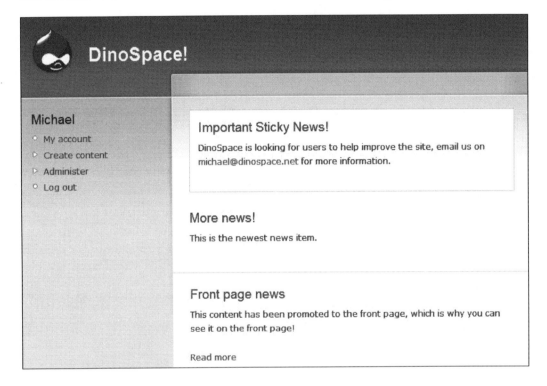

Collaboration

Drupal supports multi-user collaboration easily. It allows the content to be created, edited, and commented upon by multiple users, depending on how it is configured. Users can also share files and images, and also contact each other privately. These basic collaborative tools are built-in to Drupal, but their usefulness to our site depends on how we configure them.

Terminology

Drupal makes use of a technical vocabulary that has been documented in detail. Although I've tried to explain new phrases, words, and concepts which occur throughout the book, there may be some which I have neglected to cover in as much detail as they deserve. A detailed list of Drupal terminology is available online at `http://drupal.org/node/937`.

Administering Drupal: an overview

In order to build our site, we need to be familiar with the Drupal administration area, so let us take a look at the administration functionality within Drupal.

At this stage, it is important to note that since this book is focusing on creating a social networking site, and using Drupal as a platform to do this, we cannot go into as much detail as deserved by the various features of Drupal. We will of course, cover everything that we need to, in enough detail to use it successfully. If you would like more detail, I would recommend *Building Powerful and Robust Websites with Drupal 6*, by David Mercer (also published by Packt Publishing).

Logging in

We need to be logged in to access the administration tools; the log in box is on the left-hand side of our Drupal installation.

Once we have entered our **Username**, **Password**, and clicked **Log in**, the side menu changes to include our username and various new links appear, including the link to the administration tools.

The administration area within Drupal is broken down (by default) into five main categories, as well as a help section. They are:

- **Content Management** for managing the web site's content
- **Site building** for controlling the look and feel of the web site, as well as managing menus and modules
- **User management** to manage users, groups, and access permissions
- **Site configuration** to edit the basic configuration options for the web site, most of which we looked at in Chapter 1
- **Reports** to view reports generated by various system logs

All of these are going to play a very important role, both in the setup and the ongoing running of our site. Before looking at these in more detail, there are a few points to be noted about the administration section.

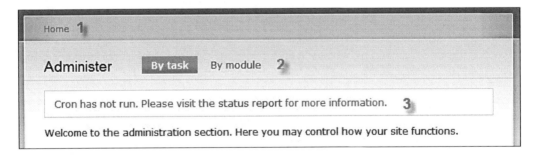

The first point, indicated by the **1** on the screenshot, is the breadcrumb trail, which allows us to easily navigate through the administration area. If we were in the post settings page, which is part of the content management section, the breadcrumb would provide us with handy links back to both the content management section and the main administration pages.

The second point is the contextual menu for the page we are currently on. In this case, it is the main administration page; so this allows us to toggle the way the options are displayed. Different areas of the administration system provide different options on this area of the screen.

The third point is a notice informing us that **Cron has not run**. This means that various scheduled tasks have not been completed, which should have been completed automatically, using either the Cron system within a Linux/UNIX hosting environment, or the Windows task scheduler. Since we have not yet set up our scheduled tasks to run, this is understandable. We could follow the provided link, and run these tasks manually if we so wished. But we will look into setting them up properly in Chapter 9, *Deploying and Maintaining our Site*.

Messages are not always displayed, but when they are, they are generally either in red to indicate an error or a warning, or in green to indicate that they are for information. Now, onto the administration sections within Drupal:

> As we go through these administrative options, why not have a think about how they can relate to your site (or to our DinoSpace site), which will be useful when we plan our site's content later in this chapter.

User management

Since we will be creating a social networking web site, the most important aspect of our web site will be our users. So let's start with the **User management** section. Most of the web site should revolve around their content, their contributions, and their connections with each other.

Access rules

With a large amount of spam being posted on web sites and a number of troublesome users using the Internet, it is important to try and protect our site. Access rules allow us to set values for usernames, emails, and hosts to which we allow or deny access to our web site. This may just involve blocking specific blocks of users or email addresses (for instance, there are a number of Russian domains, which are commonly associated with spam), blocking users from entering inappropriate words into their username, or to try and prevent a troublesome user from returning to the site.

Rules can be added from the **Add rule** link on the context sensitive menu, and consist of **Access type (Allow or Deny)**, **Rule type** (the data to check against the mask) and the **Mask**. Selecting **Deny**, **E-mail**, and then entering the domain of a spam email service such as `%@somespamemailservice.ru` would then prevent anyone from signing up with an email address from that site. However, if we also wanted to allow a specific user to sign up from that domain, we could enter their address as an allow rule.

Using the **Check rules** link, we could then enter that email address, and check that the rules would in fact allow this address.

Permissions

Permissions define the actions various users can do on our site. Users are grouped into roles, which indicate their role within the web site (for instance someone who assists us with the running of the site by editing the content, may have a role called Content Editor). This section allows us to grant permissions for various tasks to particular roles.

Permission	anonymous user	authenticated user
block module		
administer blocks	☐	☐
use PHP for block visibility	☐	☐
comment module		
access comments	☐	☑
administer comments	☐	☐
post comments	☐	☑
post comments without approval	☐	☑

In the given screenshot, you can see that the authenticated users (users who log in, and are assigned the authenticated user's role) can access comments and post comments, whereas anonymous users (users who are not logged in, and are assigned the anonymous user role) cannot.

Once we have our site set up, and decided how our visitors should contribute to our site, we shall return to look at these in more detail. The list of permissions available changes with the installation of more modules. So it wouldn't be worthwhile editing these now, if we are going to add more permissions, which we will subsequently need to grant to our users, soon.

Roles

As I've just explained, users are grouped into roles, which have privileges granted to them as defined by the user permissions.

The roles section here allows us to easily edit the permissions of a specific role, create new roles, and delete existing roles.

 The two roles available by default cannot be removed as they are an integral part of Drupal.

Name	Operations	
anonymous user	locked	edit permissions
authenticated user	locked	edit permissions
test	edit role	edit permissions
	Add role	

As you can see, new roles can easily be created simply by entering a name in the text box and clicking the **Add role** button. Similarly they can easily have their name changed or have it deleted via the **edit role** link, or have their permissions altered via the **edit permissions** link.

User settings

These settings allow us to decide if (and how) a user can register, the guidelines for registration (terms and conditions, or just some instructions), the contents of emails that are automatically sent to the users (such as when they register, when they forget their password and so on), and if user signatures and pictures are enabled.

The **User registration settings** determine if users can sign up (or if an administrator must sign them up), if administrator approval is required, and if they need to validate their email addresses.

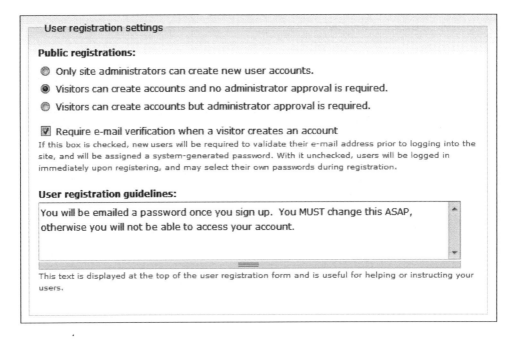

If email verification is required, the user will be emailed a password generated by Drupal. If they don't change this password, then their accounts could become inaccessible, which is why I've added a notice to the users signing up to reiterate the importance of changing their passwords once they have been sent a temporary one.

Because we are creating a social networking site, we want to encourage our users to join, and make this a simple process. So here, we should use the **Visitors can create accounts and no administrator approval is required** option.

Users

We can actually manage the users themselves via this section as well as create new users.

The **Update options** drop-down allows us to:

- Unblock users
- Block users
- Add roles to users
- Remove roles from users

Clicking a user's name from the list takes us to their profile, but at the moment, these profiles don't look particularly exciting, as you can see in the following screenshot:

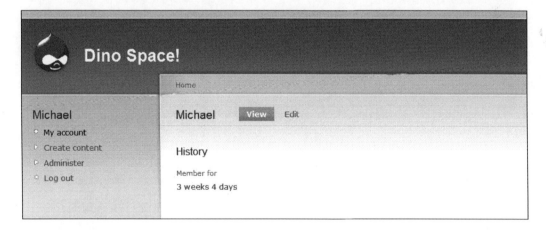

Thankfully as we progress through this book, this is one of the areas which we will improve upon.

Content management

The content management tools allow us to manage the content on our web site, and are therefore one of the most important sections of the administration area, providing us with settings and tools for:

- Comments
- Content
- Content types
- Post settings
- RSS publishing
- Taxonomy

These are the tools that are used on an ongoing basis, unlike the **Site building** tools that are generally used only when setting up a Drupal site.

Comments

Users of our web site can post comments on pages besides other content. The **Comments** section is a convenient place for administrators to see an overview of comments on the site and to moderate them. Comments are either published or unpublished; comments which are published are displayed on the web site, where as unpublished comments are visible only to users with administrative permissions.

The published status of a comment is determined based on a number of possible factors, including:

- If we, as administrators, manually altered the published status
- The role of the user posting the comment
- Hooks and event triggers based on the content of the comment

We will look at the last two of these reasons later on in this book, when we look into users and permissions in more detail. However, manually setting the published status can be done from the comments section here along with various other tasks.

The context-sensitive menu (that is, the tabs, as they are generally referred to, although with the Garland theme, they don't appear very tab-like) on this page (next to the **Comments** heading) allows us to toggle between approved comments (**Published comments**) and those pending approval (**Approval queue**). Typically the purpose of unpublished comments (those within the **Approval queue**) is to review them and then decide if they are suitable to be displayed on the web site (in which case we would approve them) or not, and if they are not, we would then delete them.

The drop-down list of **Update options** allows us to publish or unpublish comments, and also delete them. Comments can be edited by clicking the **edit** link in the operations column.

Selecting a range of checkboxes

By pressing and holding the Shift key, checking a box, and then checking the last box in the range you wish to select, you can select a large range of checkboxes easily.

Content

Comments which we looked at earlier were attached to a particular piece of content such as a forum post, blog entry or a page. This content can be managed from the **Content** area of the Drupal administration section. We only have two options for the types of content available at this time, and they are **Page** and **Story**. More will become available as we enable more features and install more modules.

Content types can also be created by the administrator directly, not just by installing new modules.

Besides published or unpublished, there are several other possibilities for the content status. There is a handy filter option available which allows us to specify the types of content or the content of the status that we wish to display. This filtering is done via the **Show only items where** section. We looked at these in detail earlier in this chapter. They include: published or not published, promoted to the front page or not promoted, sticky or not sticky.

By checking the check box next to a content element and then by clicking the **Update** button, we can perform one of the actions chosen from the **Update options** drop-down list, which includes the ability to:

- Publish the content
- Unpublish the content
- Promote the content to the front page
- Demote the content from the front page
- Make the content sticky
- Remove the "stickiness" from the content
- Delete the content

We may also be able to perform more actions, as other modules can add new actions to that list.

You may have noticed that we cannot create new content from the content area of the administration section. We will look at creating content later in this chapter.

Content Types

Content within Drupal is classified into various types (nodes), which can be managed, and new types can be created. Various modules also introduce their own content types (for example, Drupal's e-Commerce modules introduce content types such as products).

This section lists the **Content types** available, allows us to edit and delete the **Content types** and allows us to add new **Content types**.

| Content types | List | Add content type |

Below is a list of all the content types on your site. All posts that exist on your site are instances of one of these content types.

Name	Type	Description	Operations
Page	page	A *page*, similar in form to a *story*, is a simple method for creating and displaying information that rarely changes, such as an "About us" section of a website. By default, a *page* entry does not allow visitor comments and is not featured on the site's initial home page.	edit delete
Story	story	A *story*, similar in form to a *page*, is ideal for creating and displaying content that informs or engages website visitors. Press releases, site announcements, and informal blog-like entries may all be created with a *story* entry. By default, a *story* entry is automatically featured on the site's initial home page, and provides the ability to post comments.	edit delete

Initially, we only have options for **Page** and **Story** content, both of which are very similar in purpose but (by default) have some slight differences including the ability to post comments, or for the content to be promoted to the home page of our site (referred to as the front page within Drupal).

We don't need to create or edit a content type yet, both of which involve a large number of options and settings, so let's leave that for now and return to it when we need to.

Post settings

Because some pages, such as the home page, can have a number of different stories posted on them, we have some settings available to help manage this.

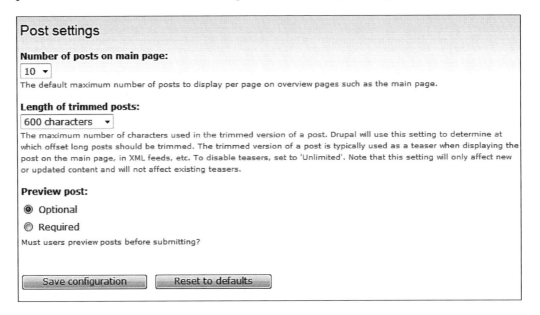

The **Number of posts on main page** setting limits the number of posts displayed on the page, the **Length of the trimmed post** setting allows us to set how much of a post is displayed on the page. If we were to display **10** posts on a page, each of which was a few thousand words long, we would have a problem! The default settings are ideal; they display a range of posts, but only provide a snippet of information (accompanied with a link to the post in full of course!).

Finally, we have the **Preview post** setting. When a post is created, the user has the option of previewing the post before submitting it. This allows the users to check if it displays correctly, and review it before submitting it. Here, we can decide if users should preview their posts or if the preview feature is just an optional extra for them to use. If preview is required, the submit button isn't shown until the submission has been previewed.

RSS publishing

By default, Drupal sites produce their own RSS feeds, the most important one is the feed of the front page content, which is available at `http://localhost/drupal-6.2/rss.xml`. There are two simple settings available for the publishing of RSS feeds by Drupal.

What is RSS?

RSS stands for **Really Simple Syndication.** One of its particular uses is to allow visitors to read blogs, posts, news items and so on, from their favorite web sites at their convenience, all in one place with a news reader application. One example of such an aggregation of lots of feeds is www.drupal.org/planet. Here, Drupal-related news from various sources is aggregated in one place using the RSS feeds from the various web site sources. For more information on RSS, Wikipedia has an extensive article: http://en.wikipedia.org/wiki/Rss.

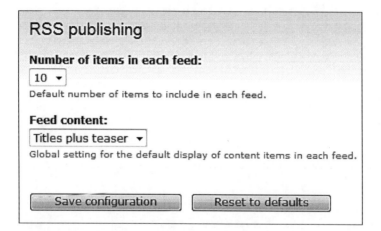

These settings are similar in nature to the **Post settings;** the **Number of items in each feed** setting defines how many items should be included in the feed, and the **Feed content** setting defines what information about the post should be contained in the feed such as just the title, the title and the teaser text or the entire content.

If we were to select **Full text,** then we may find entire articles and resources published on our site, appearing on other sites. This obviously deters new users from our site as our content would be widely available. By keeping this set to **Titles plus teaser,** the reader will need to follow the link back to our site to read the rest of the content, even if our content is aggregated onto other sites.

Taxonomy

The **Taxonomy** module within Drupal provides features to categorize and organize content using tags and terms we (as administrators) set.

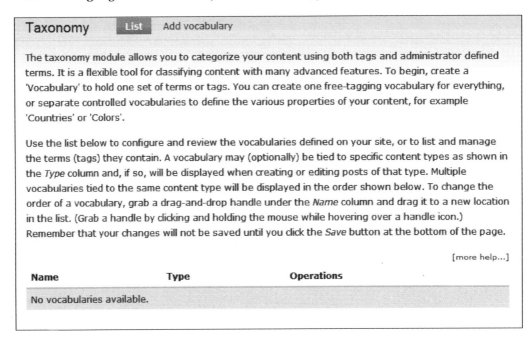

Users of our web site, provided they have the permission, can enter their own "tags" to categorize their content, or select from a list of tags which we have specified. The Drupal project web site has **Taxonomy** set so that you can categorize your post with regards to a specific version of Drupal. This has quite a number of applications and uses with regards to our site, which we will come to a little later in this chapter.

Taxonomy consists of terms (or tags) grouped into vocabularies. Vocabularies are created via the **Add vocabulary** link in the context sensitive menu, where we can define the name and description of the group of terms, set which content types can use it, and specify how it should work.

Site building

The **Site building** tools provide settings for controlling the look and feel of our site, as well as enabling additional functionality.

Blocks

Blocks provide small pieces of content, information or functionality to pages within Drupal, such as the log in box, a list of users online, and navigation. Depending on the theme being used on the site, these can be positioned in one of the following five areas on the page:

- Within the **Header**
- In the **Left sidebar**
- In the **Right sidebar**
- The **Content** pane
- The **Footer**

The blocks section in the administration tools highlights these areas of the page, so we can see where they would be displayed.

 The screenshot has been cropped so that these areas can be shown easily.

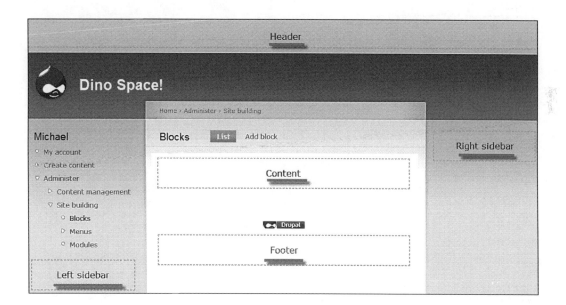

With our Drupal installation as it is, without installing any extra modules, we have the following blocks available to us:

- Navigation (the menu)
- User login (box for user to log in and display username once logged in)
- Primary links
- Recent comments (shows the most recent comments posted)
- Secondary links
- Syndicate (RSS links)
- Who's new (latest users to sign up)
- Who's online (users logged into the site at the moment)

Each of these blocks can be configured using the **configure** link in the operations column, and the region of the screen they are in can be set via the drop-down box in the sidebar.

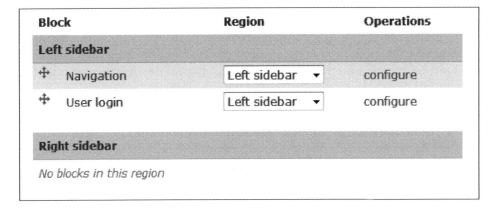

To change where the blocks are displayed, another alternative is to click the 'handle' icon, and then drag-and-drop the block into the corresponding region listed on the page.

To save the block positions after altering them this way, we need to click the **Save** button, as moving the items on their own does not save the changes. Configuring a block allows us to change the title of the block, and change which areas of the site the block appears on. Some modules automatically install new blocks; so if you return to this area later and discover new blocks you didn't add, this will be the result of additional modules.

Menus

Links to pages on our web site are grouped together in menus. These menus are listed on the menu section, and by default include the **Navigation**, **Primary links** and **Secondary links**. The navigation menu is the main menu for the site, and dynamically changes based on the page the user is on, and the role of the current user. Primary links are commonly used to show major sections of a site. These links generally don't change, and they are typically displayed as tabs along the top of the page. Secondary links are used for less important pages such as legal notices (privacy policy, terms of use and so on). Personally, I associate secondary links with a web site's footer, where you see the links to copyright information, legal policies and so on.

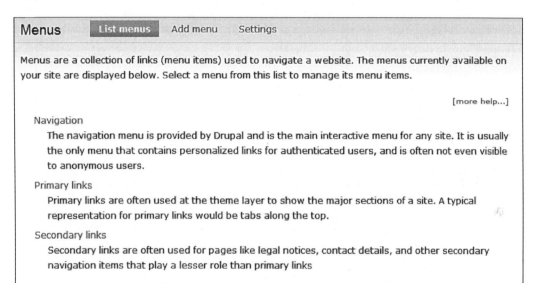

Clicking a menu from the list allows us to edit the contents of the menu, including the position of links, visibility of links, and show whether a group of links is expanded.

Expanded links: If we click the **administer** link, we have on our menu, various links related to that section appears. If the link was set to expanded, then these "sub links" would always be displayed and not only when we went to that page or one of its subpages.

The ordering of links in the menu can be edited in a similar way to the positioning of blocks, by using the 'handle' icon to drag them to new positions.

Menu item	Enabled	Expanded	Operations
✛ Compose tips (disabled)	☐	☐	edit
✛ My account	☑	☐	edit
✛ Create content	☑	☐	edit
✛ Page	☑	☐	edit
✛ Story	☑	☐	edit

The text and visibility of the menu links, their description, their parent item (to create a hierarchy of links), and their weighting can be configured from the **edit** link for each menu link.

> The weight of a link determines its order in the menu, the higher the number, the "heavier" it is, which means that it will sink further down the menu. Smaller numbers are displayed at the top.

We can use the handle icon to reorder menu links, just as with blocks.

> **Useful menu tips**
> We can also create custom menus, which get their own blocks to reside within. We can also associate a secondary menu with child elements of a main menu, to do this; we simply set the secondary menu to that of the primary menu.

Creating new menu items

To create a new menu item, we simply click the **Add item** tab when editing a menu. When creating new menu items, we need to supply the **path** of the page we are linking to. Paths are generally either `<front>` for the front page, `node/nodeid` (where `nodeid` is the ID of the node we are linking to) or a completely external web site, for example, `http://www.packtpub.com`. We can obtain the path of a page by viewing the page and making a note of the path from the address bar of our browser.

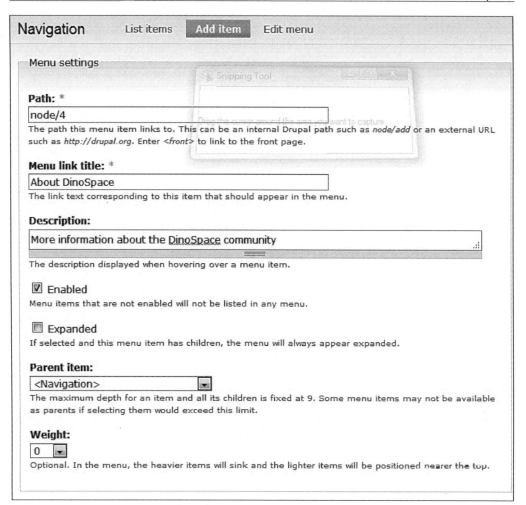

The **Menu link** title is the text we wish to display in the menu, and the **Description** is displayed when hovering over the menu item with our mouse. This description also plays a part in Search Engine Optimization (which we will look at later). So it is important to include any important, relevant keywords in there. We can also set the item as **enabled**, **expanded** to show child menu items, and specify which menu item this should be a child of, and its **weight** set to where it is positioned in the menu.

The **Parent item** field contains the other menus from within our Drupal installation. So if we were to edit a menu item, we can easily move it to another menu by changing the **Parent item** to that of an item from another menu.

Modules

Modules provide more functionality for our site, adding new features, supporting more content and enabling more interactions. New modules can be installed and enabled later, which would be listed in the modules section. By default, we have two groups of modules: **Core - required** and **Core - optional**. The **Core - required** modules are required by Drupal and cannot be disabled, whereas the optional modules are not required, but included by default (although not all are enabled by default) because they are developed by the Drupal team and are some of the most popular modules used.

By providing these features as modules, sites which don't require them don't need to use them — which helps in the efficiency of the site.

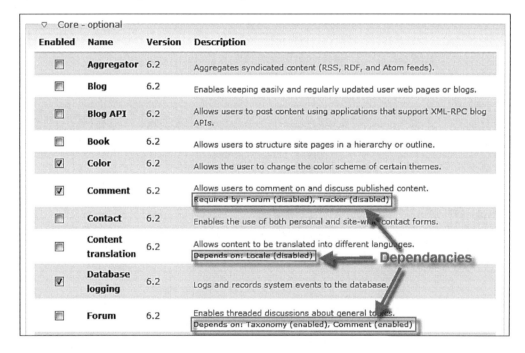

The modules listing details:

- If the module is enabled or disabled
- The name of the module
- The version of the module
- A description of the module
- Modules dependent on the module
- Modules required by the module

Modules which other modules rely on are indicated with the **Required by** text, and modules which require other modules indicate the modules they require with the **Depends on** text.

We can enable modules by checking their appropriate checkbox and then clicking the **Save configuration** button at the bottom of the page. When new modules are enabled, extra options are made available in the administration section. We don't need to enable any modules just yet, so we can leave them as they are, for now.

Themes

Themes are the design and layout of our site, and a Drupal installation can have a number of themes available. Of the installed themes, we can set one to be the default, but can have any number enabled. If more than one theme is enabled, then our users can choose the theme they wish to use.

Configuring a theme using the **configure** link allows us to alter the colors used, the logo displayed and control which page elements (such as the primary links or secondary links) are displayed.

Once we have a better idea of our web site and our audience, we will look at modifying and configuring our theme.

Site configuration

We had looked at all of these options in Chapter 1.

Reports

The reports available details information from system logs and updates which are available. Let's now look at the reports which are available.

Recent log entries

General operations such as creating and editing content, as well as administrating the site are logged by the dblog module along with system errors (such as the email sending error we received when we installed Drupal). We can see these operations and errors from this report.

user	05/31/2008 - 15:56	Session opened for *Michael*.	Michael
❌ mail	05/31/2008 - 15:56	Error sending e-mail (from ...	Anonymous
❌ php	05/31/2008 - 15:56	*mail() [<a ...*	Anonymous

Top 'access denied' errors

When a user tries to access a page which he/she is not authorized to, a log will be made in the access denied report. This may help us find links to the privileged content which we have left on our site to be clicked. Hopefully at this stage, the report should be empty.

Top 'page not found' errors

This is similar to the access denied error report, except this lists pages which users have tried to access which don't exist. Again at this stage, we shouldn't have anything in this report, although this isn't something we need to worry about now. The main advantage is when maintaining our site.

Available updates

As with most software, new and updated versions get released. With web-based software keeping up-to-date is essential, as newer versions often include fixes for any discovered security vulnerabilities. The available updates report checks to see if there are any updates to Drupal, or for any of the modules which we have installed.

Since we downloaded and installed Drupal only recently, we shouldn't have any updates available at this stage.

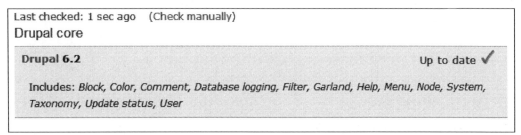

Status report final

This is the final report which checks a number of aspects of our system to ensure that everything is running smoothly and securely. These include checking that some of our server software is the correct version, that Drupal can access certain files and so on. This report also checks the **Cron maintenance tasks**, which as we noticed earlier isn't set to run once Drupal is installed, and this is indicated in the report.

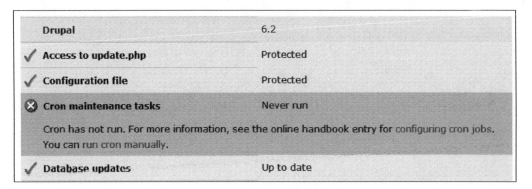

Planning our site

We now have a basic understanding of how Drupal works, and what the various aspects of its administration section do. So let's now start planning our site!

When working on new, interesting and exciting projects, such as a new web site like this one, it is often tempting to want to jump right in at the deep end and start building the site. But that would be a bad idea. If we planned our web site and its content carefully, then we should be able to offer our visitors a much better social network than we would if we just went straight into creating the site.

Let's first focus on the content we create for our site, as opposed to the content our users will create for us. This way, we can prepare the site and its preliminary content and structure, and then begin to think about how our users are going to interact and contribute. This also allows us to try and contain the non-community aspect of the site. We set up this content now, so that we can focus on our users and build a true social network in the rest of the book!

Static content

Content which isn't going to change very often is generally referred to as **static content**, and might include content such as a page describing the history of a company. For our site, a social network for dinosaur owners, the following can almost certainly be classified as static content:

- Contact us—a postal address and email address to get in touch with us, the owners of the web site
- About us—about the web site and the people behind it
- Legal information—terms and conditions, privacy policy, copyright notice, and so on.

Personally, I'm now finding it difficult to categorize any other content for this site as static content. We may wish to provide some generic information on dinosaurs, but since this is a social network, and our users are the experts, we should let them contribute to the site. So I think it is best to leave the static content limited to the information above.

Grouping content

We looked at taxonomy earlier, when we had a brief tour of Drupal's administration features and observed that it was a great way to classify content. Certain content can certainly be clearly classified with our Dinospace site, such as forum posts, pages, or generic content about specific breeds of dinosaurs. We could create tags for each specific breed such as:

- T-Rex
- Pterodactyl
- Triceratops

These terms would be grouped together as Dinosaur breed.

Starting to build our site

Now that we have a basic plan of our site's static content, we can start to build the static elements of our site.

Taxonomy!

Let's start with taxonomy. Since this is a way of categorizing content, it makes sense to set this up before we set up the content. The taxonomy options can be accessed from the menu via **Administer | Content management | Taxonomy**.

Creating the vocabulary

We need to create a new vocabulary to group the terms, which can be done via the **Add vocabulary** link in the context-sensitive menu.

The first piece of information we need to enter is to identify the vocabulary:

- **Vocabulary name**
- **Description**
- **Help text**

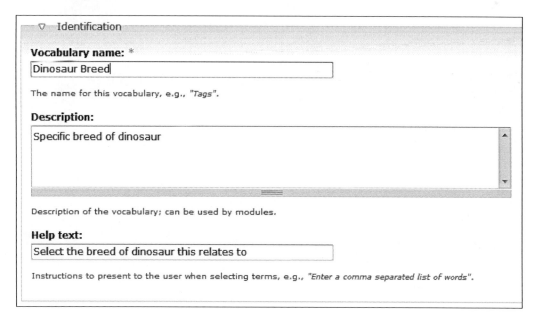

Let's enter **Dinosaur Breed** for the name, a **Description** of a **Specific breed of dinosaur** and **Help text** for **Select the breed of dinosaur this relates to**.

Next, we need to select the **Content types** which this vocabulary is available for.

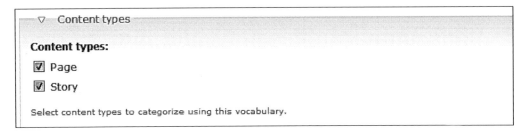

I would imagine it would be possible for both pages and stories to be related to specific breeds of dinosaurs, so let's enable those.

Next, we have some generic settings for the vocabulary, which include:

- **Tags** — which if enabled provide the users a box to enter their own tags into, separated by a comma
- **Multiple select** — which allows multiple terms to categorize content (this is always true if the tags option is checked)
- **Required** — which requires the user to select at least one term from this vocabulary for the specific type of content
- **Weight** — to determine the order of the vocabulary compared to other available vocabularies

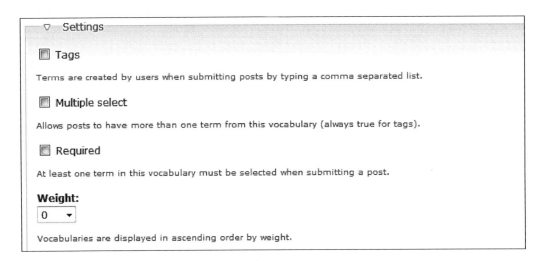

Since a page would only be related to one specific breed, we should leave the **Tags** and **Multiple select** unchecked. Some pages and stories may not even be related to a specific breed, so we don't want to require the vocabulary either. We may wish to allow multiple breeds to be selected, for instance, a user posting a story about a T-Rex eating a Brontosaurus. However, this is really a judgment call based on the site we are going to create. We can always change it later if we find a better alternative.

Creating terms and tags for our vocabulary

With our new vocabulary created, we now have some options on the main taxonomy page, next to where the new vocabulary is listed. We can edit the vocabulary, list the terms and add terms to it.

Name	Type	Operations		
Dinosaur Breed	Page, Story	edit vocabulary	list terms	add terms

We want to add new terms to the vocabulary, so let's click that.

This provides us with the option to enter a name and description for a term (a name must be entered).

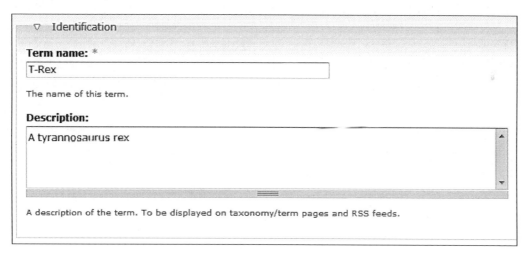

Let's enter the name of a breed of dinosaur and click **Save** before repeating the process to add the rest of the different breeds that we wish to add.

 Although we haven't seen the taxonomy in action yet, we will see it shortly when we create some content.

Creating another vocabulary—free tags

Since we may also want to categorize other content, let's create a new vocabulary called general. Only this time, we should enable the **Tags** checkbox, to allow users to define their own tags.

Creating content

Content is created from the **Create content** link on the menu.

This then takes us to a page where we can select the type of content we wish to create, which is currently only either a **Page** or a **Story**. Content types can be created for almost any purpose, including things such as a Dino Recipe, to help our users create a great meal for their pets, or a Dino Playing Cart with stats and information on specific breeds of dinosaur.

Create content

Page

A *page*, similar in form to a *story*, is a simple method for creating and displaying information that rarely changes, such as an "About us" section of a website. By default, a *page* entry does not allow visitor comments and is not featured on the site's initial home page.

Story

A *story*, similar in form to a *page*, is ideal for creating and displaying content that informs or engages website visitors. Press releases, site announcements, and informal blog-like entries may all be created with a *story* entry. By default, a *story* entry is automatically featured on the site's initial home page, and provides the ability to post comments.

Let's select **Page** so that we can create the About us page.

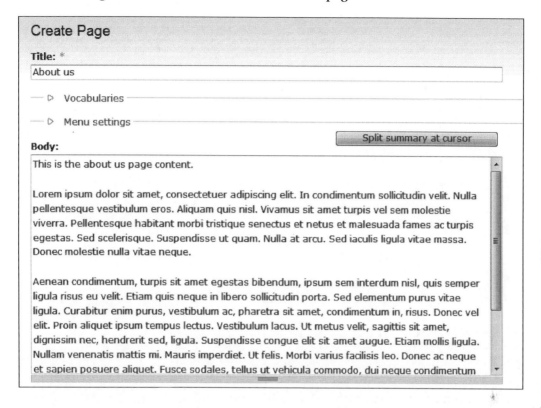

In addition to entering content such as the **Title** and **Body**, we can also define the vocabulary settings, **Menu settings** and other settings for the page. The **Split summary at the cursor** button allows us to set the text above the cursor as a teaser (which is actually a snippet of content displayed on promoting the content to the front page), or on RSS feeds. If we select the **taxonomy settings**, we can see our two new vocabularies, where if appropriate we could select a breed of dinosaur, or enter a general tag for the content.

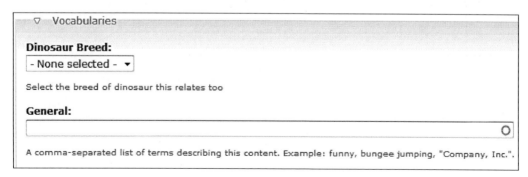

The other settings available for the content are:

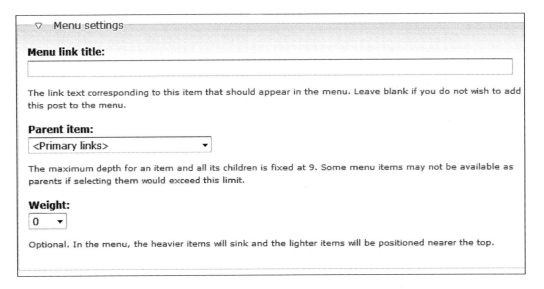 The menu option is quite important, so let's have a brief look at this now. We can't do a great deal with our sites menu at the moment as we only have provisions for some basic content (we will return to the menus later when we have our dynamic and user contributed areas all set up and ready).

▽ Menu settings

Menu link title:

The link text corresponding to this item that should appear in the menu. Leave blank if you do not wish to add this post to the menu.

Parent item:

<Primary links> ▾

The maximum depth for an item and all its children is fixed at 9. Some menu items may not be available as parents if selecting them would exceed this limit.

Weight:

0 ▾

Optional. In the menu, the heavier items will sink and the lighter items will be positioned nearer the top.

Here, we can enter a name for the **Menu link title**, and select the **Parent item** in the menu. If we wanted this page to appear on the navigation menu, without a page as its parent, we would just select `<Navigation>` from the **Parent item** drop-down list, which then gives us a menu as shown in the following screenshot:

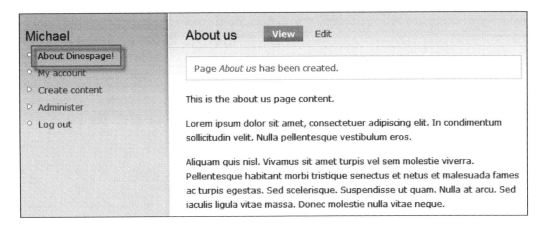

Michael

- About Dinospage!
- My account
▷ Create content
▷ Administer
- Log out

About us   View   Edit

Page *About us* has been created.

This is the about us page content.

Lorem ipsum dolor sit amet, consectetuer adipiscing elit. In condimentum sollicitudin velit. Nulla pellentesque vestibulum eros.

Aliquam quis nisl. Vivamus sit amet turpis vel sem molestie viverra. Pellentesque habitant morbi tristique senectus et netus et malesuada fames ac turpis egestas. Sed scelerisque. Suspendisse ut quam. Nulla at arcu. Sed iaculis ligula vitae massa. Donec molestie nulla vitae neque.

Try it yourself

We have created our first page! Why not try creating a few yourself? Remember earlier we looked at blocks and menus? Why not create a few pages for our secondary menu (such as copyright page, terms and conditions page, and so on) and place the menu in our site's footer?

Summary

In this chapter, we looked at Drupal in more detail, particularly at how to use its administration options which should help us in building our site. This should prove to be a useful reference point in future. We also planned some of the static content for our site, and started to create this content for it.

Our Drupal site is now ready to become a social networking site! We can now move forward with more interactive and dynamic features.

3
User Content: Contributions, Forums, and Blogs

We now have our Drupal installation ready to start becoming a social networking site! One key element of social networking sites is user generated content and that is what we will look at in this chapter. Drupal contains a number of core modules (modules which come with Drupal as opposed to modules written by others which we need to download and install) that allow our site to support user-generated content. In this chapter, you will learn the following:

- Enabling and managing user contributions as well as file attachments
- Setting up and managing discussion forums
- Giving each user a blog with the blog module
- Allowing collaborative writing with the book module
- Running polls with the polls module
- Generating content automatically with the aggregator module
- Generating content automatically in a more social way with the Feed API (this is a contributed module, which we will have to download and install)
- More about user comments

We are also going to plan the types of users we are going to have on our site and the roles and permissions they will have. Let's start by having a look at how these relate to our site.

Our site

We are going to look at a range of modules in this chapter. But it is important to understand how these relate to our site. A number of web sites and discussion forums are now leveraging the power of **syndicated** content from other web sites. Various web sites make some of their content, such as news or blog posts, available as RSS feeds. We can make use of the aggregator module to import this content into our site, providing our users with additional resources to keep them on our site, instead of seeking news and information elsewhere.

Provided we set up the permissions accordingly, any type of content such as pages, forums and blogs can be commented on by the other users. We will look at how to use the comment system to allow users to comment on contributions which help promote discussions and communication.

Users can also contribute to our site by posting other forms of content. We will look at how to enable this, and also how to enable users to upload files with their contributions, creating a more content- and media-rich experience.

With blogging becoming more and more popular, we can offer a blog for our users, directly from our site. This could be supplementary to a blog they may already have (such as to track issues specific to their dinosaur) or could become their primary blog. Having their own area of the site, the users will be more inclined to continue visiting the site as they have already spent time and energy in creating their own blog and in making contributions.

By allowing users to work together for building up the content of the site, we will find that they are more inclined to continue using the site (along with their own blog). They can also work together to contribute to the content of our site. The collaborative book module provides an excellent way for different groups of users to work together, builds up the content of the site, makes them feel like they are a part of the site's operations, and also makes our site a better and more useful place for other users as well.

Polls can allow us to gauge user feedback about our site, and also help us to find out information such as a favorite breed of dinosaur, or the average age of our users just for fun.

User roles: an important note

Different actions, such as posting a comment, posting a forum post, or uploading files require appropriate permissions. It is easier to set up all these features first, and then configure the permissions later. So for the course of this chapter, we will test out these features with our own administrative user account.

In this chapter, we will think about the different roles which might be appropriate, so that in the next chapter, we will know the appropriate permissions and roles needed to allow our users to contribute to the site. We won't focus too much on the details of how these permissions and roles work, as we will look at them in detail in the next chapter. However, at the end of this chapter, we will have a site complete with collaborative features for our users as well as permissions in place for users to be able to use the site as planned.

Drupal modules

All the features we are going to look at in this chapter are provided via modules, which we need to enable. Let's enable all these modules now to save us some time later, so we don't need to come back again and again to this section.

> Modules which are not included with Drupal need to be both downloaded and installed. These are called **contributed modules**. Since the modules we are wishing to use are part of the Drupal core, they only need enabling; we don't have to download anything at this stage.

Modules are managed from the **Administer | Site building | Modules** page. This page lists all the modules that are installed, regardless of whether they are enabled or disabled.

We need to enable the following modules from the Core—optional group of modules. Some of which are illustrated in the following screenshot:

Enabled	Name	Version	Description
☑	**Aggregator**	6.2	Aggregates syndicated content (RSS, RDF, and Atom feeds).
☑	**Blog**	6.2	Enables keeping easily and regularly updated user web pages or blogs.
☑	**Blog API**	6.2	Allows users to post content using applications that support XML-RPC blog APIs.
☑	**Book**	6.2	Allows users to structure site pages in a hierarchy or outline.
☑	**Color**	6.2	Allows the user to change the color scheme of certain themes.
☑	**Comment**	6.2	Allows users to comment on and discuss published content. Required by: Forum (disabled), Tracker (disabled)

- Aggregator—for automatically generated content
- Blog—to allow users to have their own blog
- Blog API—to allow blog users to post entries to their blog from third-party applications

- Book — to enable collaborative writing
- Comment (should already be enabled) — to allow users to comment on content
- Forum — to enable discussion board features
- Poll — to enable user polls
- Upload — to allow users to attach files to content

To enable them, we just need to check the relevant checkboxes and then click **Save configuration** at the bottom of the page.

Once the modules have been enabled, we are shown a confirmation message at the top of the page, to confirm that those modules have been enabled.

The configuration options have been saved.

Now, we can configure and use the new modules!

Comments

In Chapter 2, we looked at all the aspects of Drupal's administration, including **comments** and their moderation. Now, let us look at how the comments are created, and how we can enable them.

When creating content for our site (via the **Create content** link on the menu), there is a group of options for the content's **Comment settings**. This allows us to set whether comments are **Disabled** for that content, if they are **Read only** (useful if we need to close our discussion later on), or enabled (**Read/Write**).

Because social networking sites rely on user contributions, collaborations, and communications, we will almost always want to enable comments on content. With comments enabled, we have a link on the page to add new comments.

The comment form picks up our username, and has options for a title and the comment itself. If our users leave the title blank, Drupal will take part of the comment as the title.

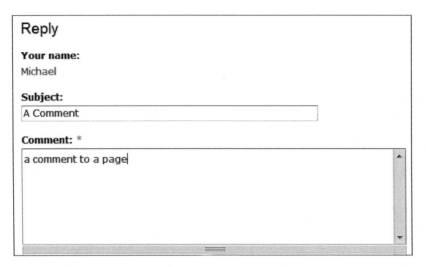

Comments within Drupal are threaded, that is, you can comment on a comment, which is great because it enhances the experience of discussion and communication—just what we need for our social network! It is clear that when a comment is a response to another comment by the style of the comment, it will be indented and displayed below the comment to which it is a response.

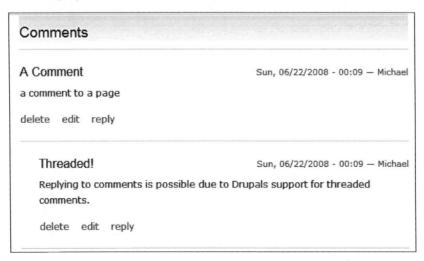

Comments within Dino Space

Comments are clearly a fundamental communication feature for any site which facilitates user interaction. However, these features can be easily abused by spammers. To help protect against spam, we should only allow logged-in users to post comments. But all logged-in users should be allowed to do this.

 Allowing only logged-in users to post comments isn't a solution to spam. We will cover more effective methods to protect against spam later in this book.

By requiring users to sign up and log in before allowing them to comment, we can hopefully encourage them to visit again as they can receive email notifications to further comments and also receive emails from us as site administrators.

Forums

Within Drupal, **discussion forums** are similar to pages with comments. A user creates a topic, and then other users can write comments on the topic. These comments are threaded in style as were comments on a particular page.

Planning

For our Dino Space site, we want to facilitate discussions on:

- Health
- Care
- Places to visit
- Dinosaur-friendly hotels
- General forums
- Stories

So let's break this down into categories which we might want to group these forums into!

- Health and Care (containing forums for health and care)
- Out and about (containing forums for places to visit, dino-friendly hotel reviews, and a general forum for other things related to getting out and about with your dinosaur)
- General (containing general dinosaur-related discussions, and discussions not necessarily related to dinosaurs)

Creating and managing forums

In the **Administration** section, we have a new link called **Forums,** which appeared once we enabled the forum module. Clicking this link takes us to the forum administration options.

> Forums
> Control forums and their hierarchy and change
> forum settings.

From here, we can control the hierarchy of forums, change the forum settings, edit and delete forums, and create forums and containers. **Forums** are used to store and organize **topics**, and **containers** can be used to store and organize forums (although a forum does not have to be stored in a container). Containers can store only forums; they can't store topics themselves, and as such are not strictly required when setting up forums.

The context-sensitive menu provides us with links to create new containers, create new forums, and alter the settings for the module. The overview page (accessed via the **List** link) allows us to manage existing forums and containers (of which we have none at the moment).

Forums	List	Add container	Add forum	Settings

This page displays a list of existing forums and containers. Containers (optionally) hold forums, and forums hold forum topics (a forum topic is the initial post to a threaded discussion). To provide structure, both containers and forums may be placed inside other containers and forums. To rearrange forums and containers, grab a drag-and-drop handle under the *Name* column and drag the forum or container to a new location in the list. (Grab a handle by clicking and holding the mouse while hovering over a handle icon.) Remember that your changes will not be saved until you click the *Save* button at the bottom of the page.

[more help...]

Name	**Operations**

There are no existing containers or forums. Containers and forums may be added using the add container and add forum pages.

To create a container for some of our forums, we need to click the **Add container** link, where we will then be asked to provide information for creating the container. We only need to enter a name for the container and select the **Parent** item. If we want to do so, we can also enter a **Description** and give it a weight to determine the order in which it is displayed on the page. If we select **<root>** as the **Parent**, then it appears on the forums page, otherwise we would need to select another container or forum for this container to appear within.

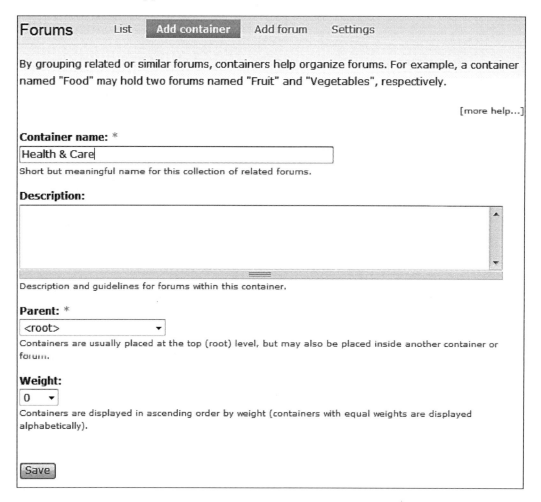

Once we have our container created (click the **Save** button to create it!), we can now create our forum which will be part of this category.

 You can create the forum first if you wish, but then you have to go back and edit it to select the parent item. This way is more logical, as we don't need to go back to the previous stages!

The options for creating the forum are the same as with the container. The difference is that when our forum is created, we can store topics within it, whereas containers can't contain topics on their own.

Let's call this one **Health and Illness** to go within our new **Health & Care** category.

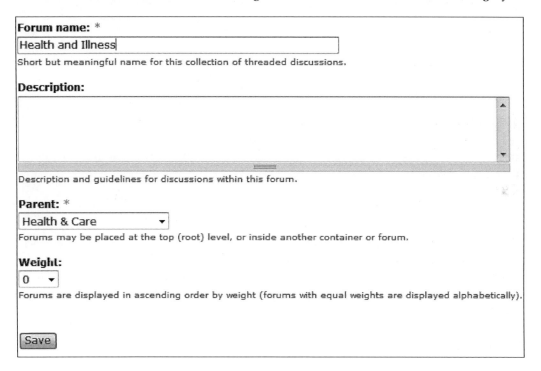

Once we have our forums created, we can click them from the overview page in the forum administration area, which takes us to the forums page (`http://localhost/drupal-6.2/forum`). We don't yet have a forums link in our menu. One was created for us automatically, but it is a suggested menu item, and needs to be enabled from the menu settings.

Forums

Post new Forum topic

Forum	Topics	Posts	Last post
Health & Care			
✉ Health and Illness Health care tips and discussion	0	0	n/a
✉ Caring for your pet dinosaur	0	0	n/a

The forums page lists the forums and the containers they are contained within as well as the number of topics and posts within each forum and the date of the last post made. Clicking a **Forum** lists all the topics within (none at the moment!), and clicking on a container takes us to a page just listing the forums within that container.

Creating a forum topic

At the top of the forum page, there is a link to **Post new Forum topic**, which allows us to create a new forum topic. If we are on the main forum page, we will need to select the forum to create the topic in; if we are within a forum, it automatically picks up the forum to post it into. Alternatively, we can click **Forum topic** from the **Create content** menu.

Topics need a subject (which is displayed on the forums page), a forum (to be displayed within), and a body (the actual content of the topic).

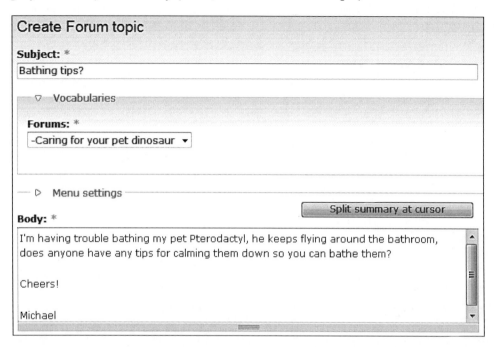

Clicking the **Save** button at the bottom of the page then creates the topic and allows other users to comment on the topic and generate discussion.

Taxonomies

If you remember, in Chapter 2, we created a vocabulary of dinosaur breeds in order to help us categorize content. The reason that we were not asked to select a dinosaur breed when creating a forum topic is because we needed to assign the vocabulary to this type of content.

We need to go to **Administer | Content management | Taxonomy**, where we can see the **Dinosaur Breed** vocabulary we created earlier. There is also a new vocabulary which was automatically created by the forum module, which contains each forum as a term. We need to click the **edit vocabulary** link next to the **Dinosaur Breed** vocabulary, and from here, we can select **Forum topic** as a content type the vocabulary can be used on.

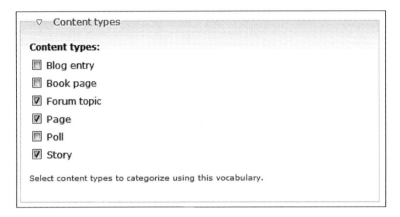

On selection, we need to click the **Save** button at the bottom of the page to update the vocabularies settings. With that updated, we now have the option to select a **Dinosaur breed** when creating a forum topic.

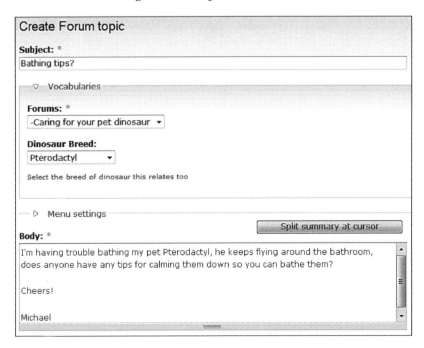

This allows us and our users to categorize the content further, making the site more organized and relevant.

If we change the taxonomy setting above to also enable polls, then we can create polls within forums too. One of the great features of Drupal forums is that we can store any content type within a forum, making them more interesting and useful to our users.

Planning: How will roles fit in?

Let's think about how we might allow our users to use the forum. Although we wouldn't want guests to be able to post topics or replies as they do with their comments, we would want all registered members to be able to contribute. We may have some users who want to help out more with the running of the site, and so, we may wish to allow them to edit and delete any topic, and help act as a moderator for the site. We may also have another group of users who can create new forums—these would of course need to be very trusted users.

Here, we can see that we may have a need for one group of users, who are very active on the site, and another group, who are trustworthy, to help grow the site.

Blogs

Apart from user permissions (which we will cover in Chapter 4), there is very little configuration available for user blogs. Once the module is enabled, our users can utilize their own blogs.

A blog can be a great way to engage communities. For our Dino Space site, we could use it as a way for our members to record what they are doing with their pet dinosaurs on a day-to-day basis, or they might just want to use it as a way to let other members know what they are doing.

 In Chapter 4, we will also be looking at allowing our users to change the design of their blogs. This will allow our users to select designs which reflect their personality or interests better, should they wish to change it.

Blog menu

Although the blog is enabled and usable by default, it isn't very obvious where it is stored, or how to use it. To get to our blog, we need to click **My account** on the **Navigation** menu and then click the **View recent blog entries** link, which isn't ideal or convenient, especially if we want members to see and interact with one another's blogs!

To make this more intuitive, we should enable the blog menu, which is already set up. We go to **Administer | Site building | Menus | Navigation** and enable the **Blogs** menu item (and the **My blog** item if it is also disabled).

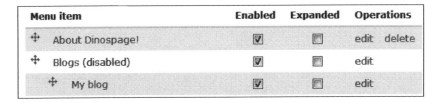

Menu item	Enabled	Expanded	Operations
✛ About Dinospage!	☑	☐	edit delete
✛ Blogs (disabled)	☑	☐	edit
✛ My blog	☑	☐	edit

Once we have checked the appropriate check boxes, we need to click the **Save configuration** button at the bottom of the page to save the changes.

Viewing blogs

The new **Blogs** link we have on the menu takes us to a page listing recent blog posts made into the various blogs on the system. This means that if we have 20 users with active blogs, this page will show the recent updates, allowing our users to stay up-to-date with what one another is doing.

Clicking the **My blog** link takes us to our own personal blog, and clicking the **username** beneath a **Blog entry** on the blogs page (for example, **Michael's blog**) takes us to their blog page.

Using the blog

To use the blog, we can click **Create content** in the navigation menu and then select **Blog entry**, which acts similar to creating pages. Or, we can visit our own blog and then click the **Post new blog entry** link.

Try it yourself: Instruction page

Why not write a help page for our users to tell them how to use their blog, and how to create entries and manage their blogs?

Blog API

The Blog API allows our users to use other applications to post blog entries, for instance, you can use Microsoft Word to write and publish a blog entry, without needing to close Word and open another program, as behind the scenes, Microsoft Word would connect to our blog using the enabled API and publish the blog entry for us.

To configure the Blog API, we need to enable **Blog entry** content types to external blogging clients. This option is available within **Administer | Site Configuration | Blog API**.

Enable for external blogging clients: *

☑ Blog entry

☐ Book page

☐ Forum topic

☐ Page

☐ Poll

☐ Story

Select the content types available to external blogging clients via Blog API. If supported, each enabled content type will be displayed as a separate "blog" by the external client.

Once the **Blog entry** checkbox has been checked, we need to click the **Save configuration** button to update the settings.

Posting a blog entry from Microsoft Word

Here is a very quick step-by-step guide for posting a blog entry directly from Microsoft Word 2007. These instructions may vary depending on your version of Microsoft Word, and also by your current setup of the software, although they can still be used as a guide. When an entry is posted, you would need to log in to Drupal to set additional options on the blog entry such as related terms and comment permissions, and so on.

1. Open Microsoft Word.
2. Create a new document, select **Blog post.**
3. If we haven't used Word to post to blogs before, we will be asked to register our account with Word. Click **Register Now**.
4. Select **Other Provider**.
5. Select **MetaWebLog API** as the API (this tells Word how it should post the entry to the site).
6. Enter `http://localhost/drupal-6.2/xmlrpc.php` as the URL and enter your username and password below.
7. Enter a title for the blog entry where it says **[Enter Post Title Here]** and enter the content for the blog below the line.
8. When finished, click **Publish**.
9. Word will then publish the entry to your Drupal blog.

Collaborative writing

Drupal's book module is designed for creating structured, multi-page content on our site, for things such as:

- Site resource guides
- Manuals
- FAQs
- An online book

Since our site is a social network for owners of pet dinosaurs, a suitable use for this module would be to allow our users to create and contribute to a book on looking after a dinosaur throughout its lifetime. Of course, as our site grows, it would be better to have more books related to specific breeds, which is something we can accommodate as our social network starts to grow!

Creating a book

The first stage in creating a new collaborative book is to create a book page which will serve as the contents page/main page for the book. We can create this page from within the **Create content** screen.

> Book page
>
> A *book page* is a page of content, organized into a collection of related entries collectively known as a *book*. A *book page* automatically displays links to adjacent pages, providing a simple navigation system for organizing and reviewing structured content.

We need to enter a title for the book, such as *Caring for your dinosaur: From egg to adult*, enter some content for this page, and then adjust the **Book outline** settings.

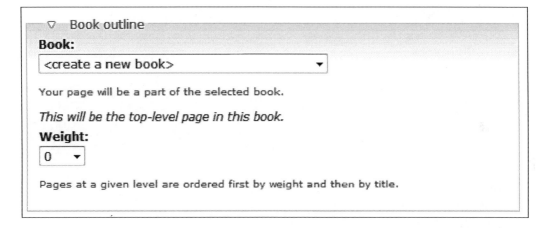

From the **Book** drop-down list, we need to select **<create a new book>**, which will then make the page the top-level page for the book.

Creating pages in the book

On our new book page, there is a link at the bottom to **Add child page**, which then takes us to the **Create Book page** screen, and within this page, the **Book outline** options have been set so that the page we were previously on is set as the **Parent item**, and the **Book** is correctly set too.

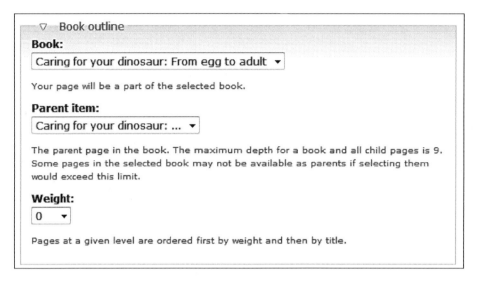

By creating a sub page, the book slowly starts to take shape, with the book's front page listing the sections of the book, and each page containing a link to the next page and the previous page to allow efficient navigation through the book.

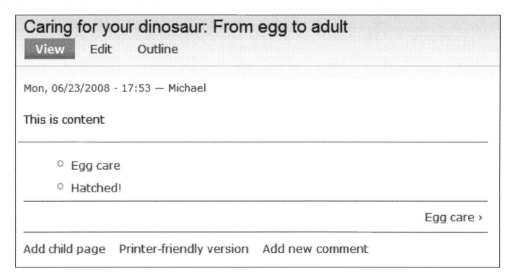

As you can see, the main page of the book lists the subsections, and has a link to the next page (**Egg care >**) at the bottom right.

Other pages contain links to the previous page on the bottom left, the next page on the bottom right, and a link to return to the top of the page in the bottom middle of the page.

‹ Caring for your dinosaur: From   up   Hatched! ›
egg to adult

Permissions and roles

This module provides great opportunity for our community members to come together, and share their knowledge on a collaborative project. There is scope for three different levels of community involvement, which would require three different roles:

- Reader—who just reads the content
- Contributor—who contributes to the books
- Commissioner/Contributor—who contributes to the books and also creates books

Why not grant all permissions?

The reason it is a good idea to separate these permissions is to prevent new users who have just signed up from diving in and contributing to certain core bits of content like this. Once a new user has established a good reputation as being responsible, we could grant them more permissions to contribute in additional areas.

Polls

Polls enable users to interact based upon simple questions. Sometimes they can be for fun, and at other times, they could be helpful in improving the web site. For instance, we could create a poll asking what the most popular area of our web site is, so that we can improve other areas or refocus content based on the replies. Alternatively, we could ask what breed of dinosaurs our users have, which would help generate some statistics for us as to which is the most popular breed. This may allow us to improve our web site.

We can create a poll from the **Create content** section, where we are then asked to enter a question for the poll and some possible answers, specify whether the poll is active (or closed), and an expiry date for when the poll should close.

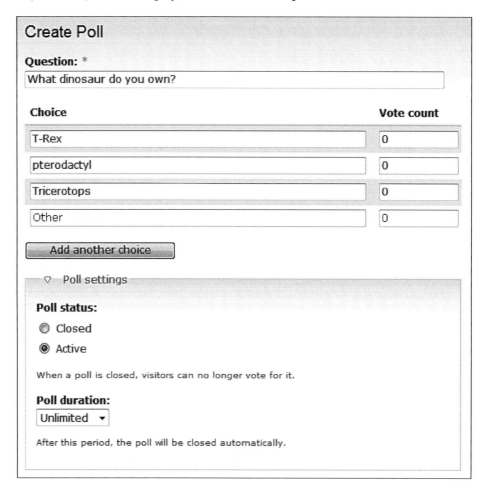

Once created, we are taken to the polls page, to which we could either link up through the menu or enable through a block of content so that it displays at the side of the site.

For now, let's try out the poll as it is.

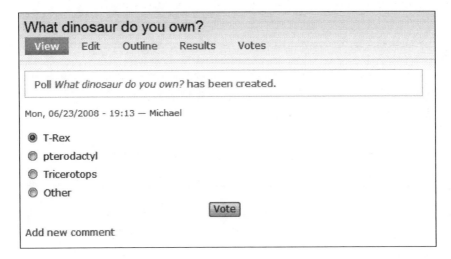

The options are displayed to our visitors to select and to vote on. Once a user has voted, they are shown the results graph that shows the percentage of votes for each option. In the following example, since only I have voted, **T-Rex** has **100%**, with only one vote:

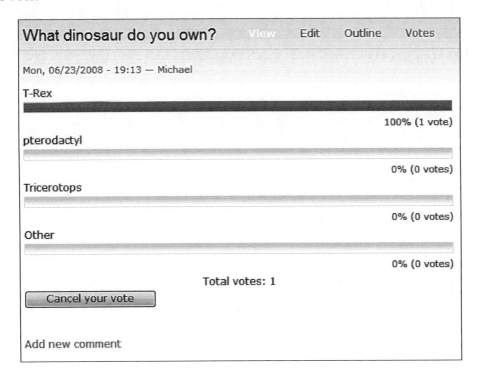

A listing of who voted for which option can be seen from the **Votes** section, which lists the usernames along with the option they voted for.

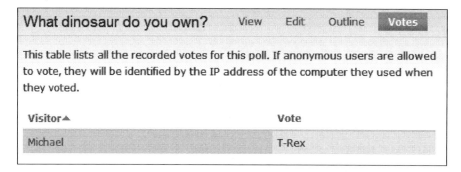

Anonymous users who vote (if allowed) are shown by their computer's IP address.

Roles

We would probably want all our registered users to be able to create a poll, and all users (not just logged-in users) to be able to vote. We may also require another group of users with the ability to edit or delete polls, should any inappropriate ones be posted.

Contributions in the form of pages

We can of course allow our users to create pages for the site too. This is something which can be done purely with roles and permissions (which we will configure in Chapter 4).

Permissions and roles

Depending on the site, we may want to allow most of our users to create pages, but we wouldn't want these pages to be shown on the front page (that is, promoted to the front page, remember that from Chapter 2?), so we may wish for another group of users to be able to promote noteworthy content.

Uploaded files/attachments

Since we enabled the **File uploads** module, we can allow our users to upload and attach files or images to content, which can be both good and bad. Thankfully, the settings available for this allow us to restrict the file types allowed, as well as the sizes of the files uploaded.

From **Administer | Site configuration | File uploads**, we can control:

- The width and the height of images uploaded (images may be scaled down automatically)
- If files should be listed as attachments with their content (if not, then they would need to be linked into their content).
- File types which are allowed (by default, only images and documents are allowed, which is more than reasonable, and I'd recommend this remain as it is; other extensions may allow users to upload virus-infected files which other users would then download)
- The maximum size of a file that can be uploaded
- The total amount of space a user can utilize with uploads

File uploads

▽ General settings

Maximum resolution for uploaded images:

| 0 | WIDTHxHEIGHT |

The maximum allowed image size (e.g. 640x480). Set to 0 for no restriction. If an image toolkit is installed, files exceeding this value will be scaled down to fit.

List files by default:

Yes ▾

Display attached files when viewing a post.

Default permitted file extensions:

jpg jpeg gif png txt doc xls pdf ppt pps odt ods odp

Default extensions that users can upload. Separate extensions with a space and do not include the leading dot.

Default maximum file size per upload:

1 MB

The default maximum file size a user can upload. If an image is uploaded and a maximum resolution is set, the size will be checked after the file has been resized.

Default total file size per user:

1 MB

The default maximum size of all files a user can have on the site.

Your PHP settings limit the maximum file size per upload to *2 MB*.

The maximum file sizes depend entirely on the amount of space and resources the site has available. If you are going to run your social network from a shared host, you may want to keep these sizes as they are. If you are planning to use a dedicated server, you may wish to increase some of the limits, depending on how many users are active on the site. These facts would need to be carefully considered at the time.

The maximum size for uploaded files is often also limited by the servers PHP settings. So if we were to increase the limit to 5Mb, we would still be limited to only 2Mb because of our PHP settings. This can be altered via the PHP configuration file. For more information, contact your web host about limits they impose, and about editing the PHP.ini file.

Automatically generated content

While this isn't technically user content, it is a very useful and important feature. If you remember, in the previous chapter, we mentioned RSS that allowed our visitors to read parts of our site through news reader programs. What the aggregator does is take an RSS feed and turn it into content. If a relevant web site has an RSS feed of news or information (and they are happy with it being displayed on third-party web sites), then we can automatically import this information onto our site.

For our Dino Space site, we may wish to automatically post content from related blogs or web sites; perhaps a Dinosaur vaccine alert web site, which posts news on Dino illnesses and their treatments.

ScienceDaily has an RSS feed related to dinosaur fossil finds, available from their web site: http://www.sciencedaily.com/news/fossils_ruins/dinosaurs/. I've created a custom feed to use in this section, which was a little more relevant to our site.

One of the new options within our Drupal administration page is **Feed aggregator** under the **Content management** category.

> Feed aggregator
> Configure which content your site aggregates from other sites, how often it polls them, and how they're categorized.

The overview of the **Feed aggregator** module shows us a list of feeds and categories currently contained within the module (there are currently none) along with the options to add a new category, add a new feed, and configure the modules settings.

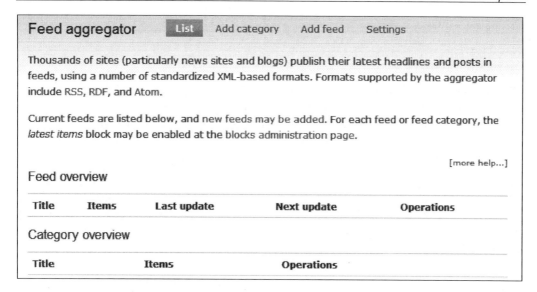

It is a good idea to group relevant feeds into categories. This will help the organization of information on the web site, especially if we end up adding a large number of feeds to the site.

At the moment, we are adding a feed related to the health of the dinosaurs (which our members may find useful), so let's create the category health. To do this, we need to click the **Add category** link and then enter a **Title** for the category. We can also add a **Description**, but this is not a required field.

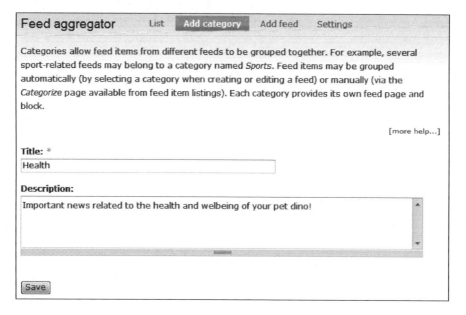

Now that we have a category which can contain our feed, we can add the feed to our site so that the content will automatically be posted!

Finding the RSS feed of a site

Web sites or blogs which have RSS feeds available generally have a link to the feed, either as text saying "RSS Feed" or "Syndicate this blog". Alternatively, it may be an image provided by FeedBurner or a small orange square with a white dot in the bottom left hand corner. Clicking the link will take you to the RSS feed; make a note of the URL of this page, as we will need it. In Internet Explorer, there is an RSS icon next to the **home page** link. If it is orange, it means that the page has a feed assigned to it, and you can click on it to see the feed.

To add the feed, we need to click the **Add feed** link, and then enter a **Title** for the feed, its **URL**, select an **Update interval** and select the categories into which the feed should be grouped.

Feed aggregator   List   Add category   **Add feed**   Settings

Add a feed in RSS, RDF or Atom format. A feed may only have one entry.

[more help...]

Title: *

    Dinosaur Disease and Infection Feed

The name of the feed (or the name of the website providing the feed).

URL: *

    http://www.peacockcarter.co.uk/ddf.rss

The fully-qualified URL of the feed.

Update interval:

    15 min   ▾

The length of time between feed updates. (Requires a correctly configured cron maintenance task.)

Categorize news items:

☑ Health

New feed items are automatically filed in the checked categories.

    Save

The **Title** is displayed on the aggregator page, and should reflect what the feed is about. So I've called this one, **Dinosaur Disease and Infection Feed**. The **URL** of the feed is the location of the feed so that Drupal can get the contents and create content from it. The **Update interval** tells Drupal how often to check to see if the feed has been updated. Let's leave this at 15 minutes for now; it won't make any difference to us yet, as we don't have cron (refer to the *Cron* section later in this chapter) tasks set up correctly. However, we can tell Drupal to manually check the feed and create content until we have cron configured properly.

Clicking **Save** then adds the feed to our site, where we can see it from the **Feed overview** area.

Feed overview				
Title	**Items**	**Last update**	**Next update**	**Operations**
Dinosaur Disease and Infection Feed	1 item	0 sec ago	*15 min* left	edit remove items update items

Category overview		
Title	**Items**	**Operations**
Health	1 item	edit

Since we told Drupal to check for updates every 15 minutes, this feed has another 15 minutes to wait before it is checked again. We can manually check for updates by clicking **update items**. All of the content which is created from a feed can be removed via the **remove items** link.

Feed aggregator menu

By default, we don't have a menu link for the feed aggregator module. To enable it, we need to go to **Administer | Site Building | Menus**. From here, we need to select the menu (Navigation), find the **Aggregator** menu link, and check the **Enabled** box to enable the menu link.

Viewing the feed in action

Clicking the **Feed aggregator** link in the main navigation menu takes us to the list of content which has been imported by our feed.

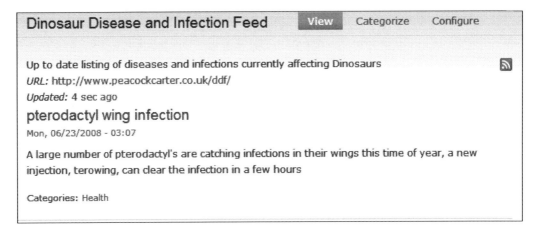

The description of the feed shown is taken from the feed itself, and cannot be changed unless you have control over the feed.

By aggregating information from a wide range of sources, we can provide up-to-date information on relevant topics which our users might benefit from or find interesting, without relying on our users to post that information directly by themselves.

Cron

Since we are not running this on a live site, we have not configured cron; this is required to pull in feeds regularly. To see this in action before we deploy the site and configure cron later in the chapter, we can manually run the cron. Cron can be manually run by visiting the `cron.php` file in our web browser.

Social aggregation

While the aggregator module is very useful, it isn't a very social feature. What would be great is if we could allow certain users to post feeds for their own web sites, or web sites they like, and have new content elements (nodes) created based on the items in those feeds.

We can do that with the FeedAPI module. This is a contributed module, which means we need to download and install it, before we can use it. Up until now, we have only used core modules, which didn't need to be downloaded first; we just had to enable them. We are going to cover installing contributed modules in much more detail later in this chapter. So let's quickly download and install this module without focusing too much on what we are doing to install it at this stage (as this will be covered in more detail shortly).

Download the module

We need to visit the Feed API project page `http://drupal.org/project/feedapi`, and download the official release which is **Recommended for Drupal 6.x**, as this ensures it will be compatible with our version of Drupal.

Install and enable the module

The file we have just downloaded is a ZIP file, which needs to be extracted (using a program such as WinZip, or the built-in application for handing compressed files), to the `sites/all/modules` folder within our Drupal installation. The `modules` subfolder may not exist, so if prompted, allow your decompression program to create this folder.

Because we have just placed the modules files within our Drupal installation, the modules should be picked up by Drupal so that we can enable them. We need to visit the modules section (**Administer | Site building | Modules**), where we can enable the modules.

Grouped under the **FeedAPI Default** heading, we can now enable the **FeedAPI** and **FeedAPI Node** modules, and the **Common syndication parser** and **FeedAPI inherit** modules (grouped under **FeedAPI Add On**) by ticking their boxes and clicking **Save configuration** at the bottom of the page.

▽ FeedAPI Default

Enabled	Name	Version	Description
☑	**FeedAPI**	6.x-1.5	Provides feed aggregation functionality, a feed management interface and an API. If you enable this module, enable at least one item processor (e. g. FeedAPI Node Item) and one parser (e. g. SimplePie parser). Required by: FeedAPI Inherit (disabled), FeedAPI Node (enabled), Common syndication parser (disabled), SimplePie parser (disabled)
☑	**FeedAPI Node**	6.x-1.5	Creates nodes from feed items. Depends on: FeedAPI (enabled) Required by: FeedAPI Inherit (disabled)
☐	**SimplePie parser**	6.x-1.5	Provides an XML parser for FeedAPI modules. Uses SimplePie library. Requires SimplePie 1.01+. Depends on: FeedAPI (enabled)

Configure the module

There are two areas within the administration tools where we can configure this module, the first is within **Administer | Site settings | FeedAPI settings**. These settings allow us to set which HTML tags are allowed in the feed elements that are posted.

The second group of settings are in **Administer | Site building | Content types | Feed**. These settings define when the items from the feed are updated, including whether a feed should be refreshed when it is created, whether existing feed items should be refreshed when a feed is updated, and whether we should pause updating a feed, and also whether we can delete feed generated content after a specific period of time.

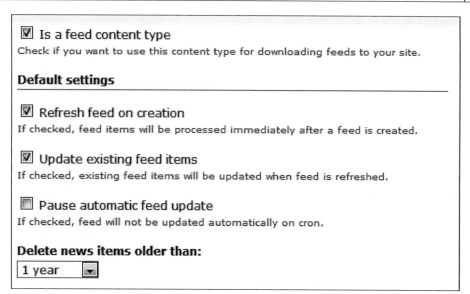

Beneath that, we have the **Parser settings** which control how the feed is processed (parsed), we only have one parser installed, and it is currently enabled.

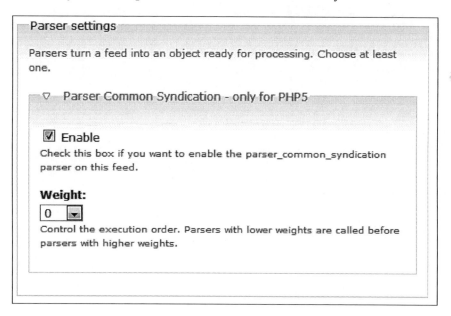

Next, we have the **FeedAPI Node – create nodes form feed items** settings. These settings define how nodes should be created from the feed content, we can also specify whether we wish to set the latest few elements in a feed as promoted to the front page.

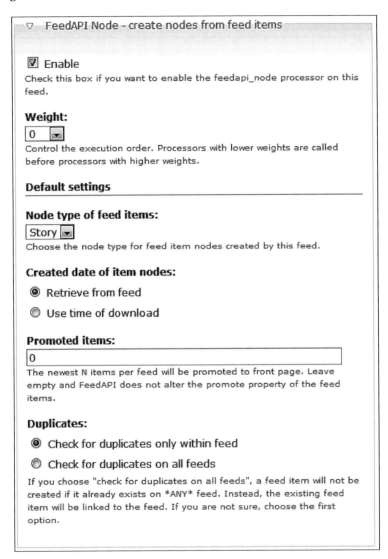

Most of these settings are shown as the defaults when creating a new feed, and can be changed by the user.

Using the module

To use this module, users can click **Create content | Feed** and create a feed by entering the **URL** of a feed. This creates a content element for the feed (the title of which is either obtained via the feed itself, or is set by the user as title at the time of creation), and new Story elements for each item in the feed (as defined by the settings).

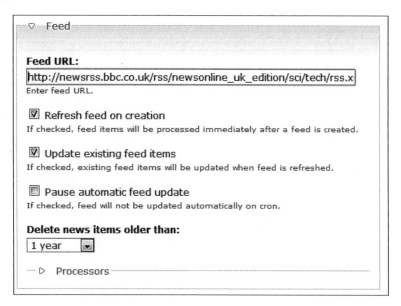

This then creates a new feed for us, as illustrated in the following screenshot:

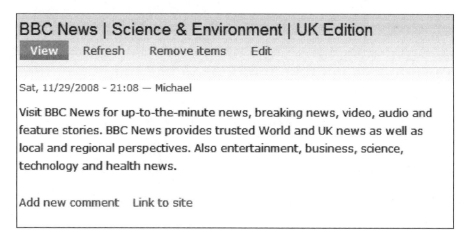

From **Administer | Content management | Feeds**, we can manage feeds which have been added to our site, edit them, delete them, and delete stories created from them.

Feeds

Current feeds are listed below. For each FeedAPI-enabled content type, the *Quick create* block may be enabled at the blocks administration page.

Averages over the last 28 days.

Title	Last refresh	New items added per update	Update rate	Number of items	Processing time	Commands
BBC News	Science & Environment	UK Edition	*1 min 8 sec* ago	29	No data yet	29	7492 ms	○ Delete ○ Remove items ○ Refresh ○ Edit

Each node created by a feed can be commented on by our users, which means that we can generate new discussions based on user submitted feeds!

We can make it easier for users to create feeds, by enabling a content block which was automatically created by the module. The block is called **FeedAPI: Quick create Feed** and is enabled via **Administer | Site building | Blocks**.

This block allows users to simply paste in a new feed link, and create a feed node which will automatically create new content based on the content in the feed, quickly.

Roles

We have two roles by default, the anonymous user role, which is the set of permissions used by anyone who is not logged in, and there is the authenticated user role for those who are logged in. We shouldn't need to change the anonymous user role much, as by default, permissions are not granted. But we will need to alter the authenticated user role to allow our users to contribute to the site. A number of new roles will also need to be created for moderators and power contributors.

 We will be looking at users, roles, and permissions in great detail in the next chapter, this is just a quick look through, so we can set up the permissions related to the new features we have installed on our site.

To alter the permissions for a role, we need to go to **Administer | User management | Roles** and then click **edit permissions** for the particular role. Permissions are then granted by checking the appropriate box on the page which follows.

Anonymous role permissions

All we need to do for this role is ensure that the permissions are granted for various view content, view feed, and view comment options.

Authenticated users

We need to check the following permissions for the authenticated user role, so they can use these new features:

- Aggregator module—Access news feeds
- Blog module—Create blog entries, delete own blog entries, edit own blog entries
- Comment module—access comments, post comments, post comments without approval
- Contact module—access site-wide contact form
- Forum module—create forum topics, edit own forum topics
- Node module—access content, create story content
- Poll module—vote on polls
- Upload module—upload files, view uploaded files
- User module—access user profiles

Creating the additional roles

To create additional roles, we go to **Administer | User management | Roles** and enter a name for a role into the text box. Click **Add role** and then set the permissions accordingly. Authenticated user role is automatically given to users who are registered, whereas other roles must be manually assigned to the users we wish to grant these permissions to.

Contributors

For users who are going to be a little more active in the running of the site, we need to set the following permissions, in addition to those of the authenticated user role:

- Book module—add content to books
- Node module—create book content, create page content, edit own book content, edit own page content, revert revisions, and view revisions.

Moderators

Moderators need the ability to edit and delete content other than their own. So, we would provide the following permissions, in addition to those of the authenticated user role:

- Blog module—delete any blog entry, edit any blog entry
- Comment module—administer comments
- Forum module—delete any forum topic, edit any forum topic
- Node module—delete any book content, delete any page content, delete any story content, delete revisions, edit any book content, edit any page content, edit any story content, revert revisions, and view revisions

Power contributors

Power contributors need to be able to create additional major content elements such as discussion forums, polls, and books. So in addition to moderator privileges and contributor privileges, we should grant the following permissions:

- Book module—administer book outlines, create new books
- Forum module—administer forums
- Poll module—create poll content

Summary

We have enabled various core modules that allow user contributions to our site, including:

- Comments
- Blogs
- Forums
- Contributions
- Attachments
- Polls

We have also set up the contributed (non-core) Feed API module.

In the process of doing this, we have thought about the various user roles we might wish to have in our social networking site! This is a very important thing to consider, as without the correct setup of roles and permissions, we may end up with a social networking web site where registered users cannot do anything (at the moment, this is the case unless they are an administrator) or where any registered user can do anything (which would give them full administrative control, which obviously, we would not want).

4
Users and Profiles

With our social networking site ready to accept user content, and our roles set up to allow groups of users to contribute to and use our network in different ways, it is time to focus more on our users–specifically, managing users and the settings associated with them, and providing them with tools and options to improve their experience on the site.

In this chapter, you will learn:

- About **Gravatars(Globally Recognized Avatars)** and how to enable them
- What Open ID is and how we can use it on our network
- How users can track the activity of each other
- How to add extra fields to user profiles
- How to allow our users to customize their own blogs
- About settings and rules for users
- More about users, roles, and permissions

What are we going to do and why?

Before we get started, let's have a closer look at what we will be doing, and why. Our users can interact with the web site, and they can have their own blog. Apart from this, there are very few provisions for the users to tell everyone else about themselves, and expand their profiles with something more personal. With a site like ours, it would be useful to know more about our users including:

- Their pet dinosaur's name
- Breed of dinosaur
- Their pet dinosaur's birthday
- The dinosaur's hobbies and so on

- Their web address (if they have one)
- Location/City/Area
- More information about the user themselves

This can be added to user profiles using the Profile module, which is a core module within Drupal, and simply needs to be enabled and configured.

Many web sites allow users to upload an image to be associated with their accounts, which could be either a small photo of themselves, or a small image known as an avatar. Drupal allows this, but it has some drawbacks which can be fixed using Gravatar. Gravatar is a social avatar service, whereby users set up their avatars, and other web sites automatically pick up their avatars by sending a request to the Gravatar service with the users' emails. This is convenient for our users, as it saves them having to upload their avatars to our site, and reduces the amount of data stored on our site as well as the data being sent and received from our site. This module needs to be downloaded, installed and configured for our users to make use of its features. With the upload module enabled, users can upload their own avatars directly to the site, if they choose to do so. This is because not all users would be members of Gravatar, nor would they all wish to sign up to a third-party service.

With the rise in the number of web sites and social networks that users of the Internet are members of, having to log in to different web sites on a daily basis can put off users if they have to sign up to another web site. OpenID helps prevent this as users need to remember only one username and password. It works by allowing users to login by providing a web address, instead of their usernames and passwords. This web site is their identity with an OpenID provider (maybe it is their own web site or another social network—MySpace and other social networking web sites are OpenID providers). When they log in with these identities, they will be taken to these web sites to log in before being returned to our site. If they have already logged in into their OpenIDs, they will return to the web site as new users. More information on OpenID is available from `http://openid.net/`. This is a core module which just needs to be enabled.

 There are two important points to be noted about OpenID. Firstly, it is decentralized, which means log in details are not tied to a specific provider, and secondly, it is offered as an alternative log in method—users without an OpenID (or those who don't know they have an OpenID!) can still log in or sign up as normal.

Users have their own blogs which they can use, but they are not personalized blogs. By installing the blog theme module, we can allow our users to select different themes for use in their blogs. This way, visitors to one particular user's blog (for example 'Bob') will see the theme that Bob chose.

Once users get to know each other more, they become more interested in each other's posts and topics, and may wish to look up a specific user's posts and contributions. The Tracker module allows users to track one another's contributions to the site. This is a core module, which just needs to be enabled and set up.

Now that we have a better idea of what we are going to do in this chapter, let's get started!

Install the modules

To make things easier for us, let's install and enable all the relevant modules first. This saves us having to do this again and again at a later stage.

The modules which we require are:

- Profile (a core module)
- Tracker (a core module)
- OpenID (a core module)
- Gravatars (`http://drupal.org/project/gravatar`)
- Blog Theme (`http://drupal.org/project/blogtheme`)

We need to download the relevant modules (ensuring we download ones which are compatible with Drupal 6.x), and extract the ZIP files into the `/sites/all/modules` folder.

 As we have not downloaded and installed any new modules on our Drupal installation yet, we will need to create the folder `modules` within the `/sites/all/` directory. The reason there are `sites/all` and a `sites/default` directories is because Drupal can support multiple web sites running off one installation, and this defines which modules are available to which of the installations. Core modules are located elsewhere, which is why we don't have a modules folder already in this location containing the core modules.

Now all the modules just have to be enabled via the **Site Building | Modules** section of the **Administration area**.

 Modules are enabled in the same way as done in the previous chapter; we just need to check the checkbox next to their names on the module listing page.

Users, roles, and permissions

In Chapter 3, we looked at the setup of some roles and assigned some permissions to the roles. Let's have a more detailed look at users, roles, and permissions and also how they work.

These are all areas of the administration area, within the **User management** section.

User management
Manage your site's users, groups and access to site features.

Access rules
> List and create rules to disallow usernames, e-mail addresses, and IP addresses.

Gravatar
> Administer how gravatars are used.

Permissions
> Determine access to features by selecting permissions for roles.

Profiles
> Create customizable fields for your users.

Roles
> List, edit, or add user roles.

User settings
> Configure default behavior of users, including registration requirements, e-mails, and user pictures.

Users
> List, add, and edit users.

The other options within this section (**Access rules**, **Gravatar**, **Profiles** and **User settings**) will be looked at later in this chapter.

Users

When a visitor signs up for our site, a user account is created for him/her. From the **Users** area, we can view a list of existing users, create new ones and edit them. Within the context of editing a user, not only can we edit their details, such as their usernames or passwords, but we can also suspend their user accounts or delete their user accounts permanently from our social network.

We want our site to become popular, which means that we want to have lots of users. When we get lots of users, it will become more difficult to navigate through their list, and this is when searching, sorting, and filtering them come in handy—which is what we are going to look at now.

For each user, the user list displays:

- The username
- The status of the user account (active or blocked)
- Roles associated with the account
- Length of time the user has been a member for
- The time passed since the user was last active on our site
- A link to edit the user

Viewing/searching/sorting/filtering

Clicking the username will take us to their user profile. We can sort the list of users by clicking the heading in any of the columns to sort the list by that column. One particular use of doing this is that we can see all blocked users, so we can quickly reactivate an account should we need to, or see who the newest members are.

We can also filter the accounts displayed using the **Show only users where** panel.

This allows us to filter the list based on whether the account is active or not, or against specific roles assigned to users.

Creating a user

At the top of the users page, we have the **Add user** link.

This takes us to the new user page, where we are required to fill out the **Username**, **E-mail address**, **Password**, and **Confirm Password** again for the user. We can also opt to notify the users of their new accounts, which will send them an email informing them that they have a new account with the Dino Space social network.

Username: *

    Richard

Spaces are allowed; punctuation is not allowed except for periods, hyphens, and underscores.

E-mail address: *

    richard@peacockcarter.co.uk

A valid e-mail address. All e-mails from the system will be sent to this address. The e-mail address is not made public and will only be used if you wish to receive a new password or wish to receive certain news or notifications by e-mail.

Password: *

    ••••••••••••••••   Password strength: High

Confirm password: *

    ••••••••••••••••   Passwords match: Yes

Provide a password for the new account in both fields.

Status:

◎ Blocked

◉ Active

☑ Notify user of new account

    Create new account

Editing

To edit an account, we just need to click the **edit** link which corresponds to the account, which takes us to the edit page.

Account information

Username: *

Michael

Spaces are allowed; punctuation is not allowed except for periods, hyphens, and underscores.

E-mail address: *

mkpeacock@gmail.com

A valid e-mail address. All e-mails from the system will be sent to this address. The e-mail address is not made public and will only be used if you wish to receive a new password or wish to receive certain news or notifications by e-mail.

Password:

Confirm password:

To change the current user password, enter the new password in both fields.

Status:

⊙ Blocked

◉ Active

We can edit the user's **Username**, **E-mail address**, **Password**, account **Status** and settings pertaining to modules, which give users additional settings too.

Careful!

If you edit these settings, the users may not be able to log in to their accounts. If you change a user's **Username** without his/her request, you should let him/her know through email.

Suspending/blocking a user

Within the edit page, we have an option entitled **Status**, which can be set to either **Blocked** or **Active**.

This would allow us to block a user from accessing our site, for instance if they had been posting inappropriate material repeatedly, even after being contacted and asked to stop.

Why block? Why not just delete?

If we were to just delete a user who was posting inappropriate material, or doing something we didn't want, then he/she could just sign up again. Blocking the user prevents him/her from signing up with the same email address and username. Of course, he/she could sign up again with a different email address and a different username. But this helps us to keep things under control.

Deleting a user

At the bottom of the edit user screen, there are two buttons: **Save** and **Delete**.

The **Save** button will confirm and save any changes made to the user's account, and the **delete** button will permanently remove the user from our social network.

When to delete a user

A user may request to be removed from the web site, in which case, we can use this feature.

Roles

As we discussed in the previous chapter, users are grouped into roles, which in turn have permissions assigned to them. By default, there are two roles within Drupal (although we have more now because of the ones we added in Chapter 3). These two roles are:

- **anonymous users**
- **authenticated users**

These roles can be edited, but they can neither be renamed nor deleted. This is why the **Operations** column in the table below is **locked**.

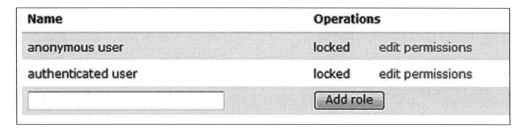

The **anonymous user** role is the role for any user who is not logged-in, and so the permissions associated with it are those which a guest user has. Whereas the role of an authenticated user suits all those users who are logged-in. Additional roles which are added can apply to any number of users. At this stage, we must select which users have which roles assigned to them. Later on in this book, we will look at how our users can change their roles and get more active within our network with features such as **Organic Groups**.

Editing the permissions of a role allows us to select which permissions are granted to users who have that role assigned to their account. New roles are simply created by entering the name of a new role into the text box and then clicking the **Add role** button and selecting the permissions to be granted to those users.

Permissions

The **Permissions** section provides us with a grid view for roles and the permissions assigned to them. All the permissions which can be granted are listed down the side (for example, create blog entries) and the roles along the top. The use of this view, if we were to install a new module with new permissions related to it, is that we could easily update all of our roles to have the desired permissions directly from the grid view.

The **Save permissions** link at the bottom of the page saves the changes made.

Adding special properties to user profiles

With the **Profile** module enabled, we now have a new section within the User management area, called **Profiles**.

> Profiles
>
>   Create customizable fields for your users.

This provides us with a number of new options to add new fields to user profiles, including:

- **Single-line text fields**
- **Multi-line text fields**
- Checkboxes
- List selections
- Freeform lists
- Web addresses
- Dates

Earlier in this chapter, we looked at how to extend the user profile in our site. Let's look at this again, but relate the options we wished to add to the types of fields that are available.

- Their pet dinosaurs' name—this would be a **single-line text field**
- Their pet dinosaurs' birthday—this would be a date
- Breed of dinosaur—this would be a list selection, with the different dinosaur breeds available from a list
- The dinosaur's hobbies and so on—this could be a **multi-line text field**, or a free form list allowing the user to either enter a lot of text or a number of different options
- Their web address (if they have one)—this would be a web address field
- Location/City/Area—this would be a **single-line text field**
- More information about the user—this would be a **multi-line text field**

Module overview

The module overview screen (the page we see when we click the **Profiles** link) lists fields which are currently set up (we don't have any at the moment) and lists the types of fields which we can create at the click of a button.

Title	Name	Type	Operations
No fields available.			

Add new field

- ○ single-line textfield
- ○ multi-line textfield
- ○ checkbox
- ○ list selection
- ○ freeform list
- ○ URL
- ○ date

Extending our users' profiles

All the different field types have very similar configuration options available, including:

- Category
- Title
- Form name
- Explanation
- Visibility
- Page title
- Weight
- Auto-complete
- Mandatory
- Visible in the user registration form

The list selection field also has an additional option. It is Selection options field, which contains the list of options the select field will have, each separated by a new line.

The first three options for the field are compulsory, and must be completed for each field that we create.

Category: *

The category the new field should be part of. Categories are used to group fields logically. An example category is "Personal information".

Title: *

The title of the new field. The title will be shown to the user. An example title is "Favorite color".

Form name: *

profile_

The name of the field. The form name is not shown to the user but used internally in the HTML code and URLs. Unless you know what you are doing, it is highly recommended that you prefix the form name with `profile_` to avoid name clashes with other fields. Spaces or any other special characters except dash (-) and underscore (_) are not allowed. An example name is "profile_favorite_color" or perhaps just "profile_color".

Different custom fields can be grouped together using the **Category** option; fields with the same category would be grouped together. The **Title** of the field would be entered in the title field, and a unique **Form name** is required for the HTML behind the field we are creating. This could just be `profile_` followed by a version of the title field but without spaces and punctuation.

Explanation:

An optional explanation to go with the new field. The explanation will be shown to the user.

Visibility:

○ Hidden profile field, only accessible by administrators, modules and themes.

○ Private field, content only available to privileged users.

◉ Public field, content shown on profile page but not used on member list pages.

○ Public field, content shown on profile page and on member list pages.

Page title:

To enable browsing this field by value, enter a title for the resulting page. The word %value will be substituted with the corresponding value. An example page title is "People whose favorite color is %value". This is only applicable for a public field.

To explain to the user what the field is for, and provide more details as to why or what is being asked from them, we can enter some information in the **Explanation** setting. The **Visibility** setting defines who can see the information relating to the user in the custom profile field:

- **Hidden** — It may be hidden, visible only to administrators; useful if we were to have a field for leaving notes about a user, for example, reasons why an account has been blocked temporarily

- **Private** — Accessible only to privileged users (users with permission to see that particular field)

- **Public** — This field is on the users profile page, but not listed on the members list

If the field was made public (the latter public option) and we wanted to view a page where a user has that option, we can enter the title for that page.

Weight:

0 ▾

The weights define the order in which the form fields are shown. Lighter fields "float up" towards the top of the category.

☐ Form will auto-complete while user is typing.

☐ The user must enter a value.

☐ Visible in user registration form.

We then have the **Weight** of the field which determines its position in the list of fields, and the auto-complete option, which if enabled, will try to guess the value of the field based on the first view characters (for example, useful for selecting the breed of dinosaur a user owns). Finally, we have options as to whether the field is mandatory, and whether the form is to be shown on the user registration page.

Single-line text fields

We want to create two custom text fields, they should be created as shown here:

Dinosaur name

- Category: About your dinosaur
- Title: Dinosaurs' name
- Form name: profile_dinosaur_name
- Explanation: The name of your pet dinosaur
- Visibility: Public (latter)
- Page title: Owners of dinosaurs called %value
- Weight: 0
- Auto-complete: No
- Mandatory: No
- Visible in the user registration form: Yes

Location

- Category: About your dinosaur
- Title: Location
- Form name: profile_location
- Explanation: Where you and your dinosaur live
- Visibility: Public (latter)
- Page title: Dinosaur owners located in %value
- Weight: 4
- Auto-complete: No
- Mandatory: No
- Visible in the user registration form: Yes

Multi-line text fields

We would have one multi-line text field as shown here:

About you

- Category: About you
- Title: About you
- Form name: profile_about
- Explanation: More information about you
- Visibility: Public (former)
- Page title: N/A
- Weight: 6
- Auto-complete: No
- Mandatory: No
- Visible in the user registration form: Yes

Date field

We would have one date field as shown here:

Dinosaur's date of birth

- Category: About your dinosaur
- Title: Dinosaurs' date of birth
- Form name: profile_dinosaur_dob
- Explanation: When was your dinosaur born
- Visibility: Public (former)
- Page title: N/A
- Weight: 1
- Auto-complete: No
- Mandatory: No
- Visible in the user registration form: Yes

List selection field

We would have one list selection field containing all of the breeds of dinosaurs as shown here:

Breed

- Category: About your dinosaur
- Title: Dinosaurs' breed
- Form name: profile_dinosaur_breed
- Selection options: T-Rex, Triceratops, etc. all separated by a new line.
- Explanation: The breed of your pet dinosaur
- Visibility: Public (latter)
- Page title: Owners of %value dinosaurs
- Weight: 2
- Auto-complete: Yes
- Mandatory: No
- Visible in the user registration form: Yes

Free form list field

We would have one free form list field for the activities which the dinosaur enjoys such as:

About your dinosaur

- Category: About your dinosaur
- Title: Dinosaurs' activities
- Form name: profile_dinosaur_activities
- Explanation: Activities your dinosaur loves
- Visibility: Public (former)
- Page title: N/A
- Weight: 3
- Auto-complete: No
- Mandatory: No
- Visible in the user registration form: Yes

Web address field

We would have one web address field that looks like this:

Your web address

- Category: About you
- Title: Your web address
- Form name: profile_url
- Explanation: About you
- Visibility: Public (former)
- Page title: N/A
- Weight: 7
- Auto-complete: No
- Mandatory: No
- Visible in the user registration form: Yes

Editing our profile

If we go to our profile (the **My account** link in the menu) now and then click **edit**, we have two new tabs containing options: **About you** and **About your dinosaur**.

About you

The **About you** section contains all of the fields in the **about you** category we created.

About your dinosaur

The **About your dinosaur** section contains the fields from the **about your dinosaur** section we created.

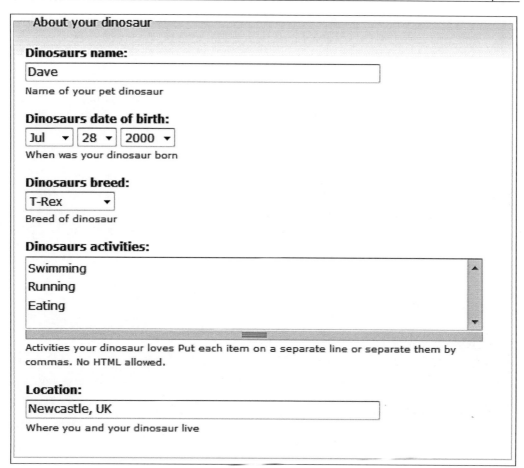

Tracking user activity

The name of this module is slightly misleading. It allows you to view the recent contributions of a user to the site.

Michael		View	Track		
Type	**Post**	**Author**	**Replies**	**Last updated**	
Page	Test Page	Michael	2	3 weeks 5 days ago	

One particular use for it, is that if one user found a particular user's posts interesting (perhaps, they both owned troublesome T-Rexes!), they could view the user's track page, and look for other contributions from that user which they might be interested in.

This is only one way of interaction though, as opposed to two users interacting with each other. We will look into users interaction with one another in Chapter 5.

Settings and rules

Within **User management**, we have three areas that we are yet to cover. They are:

- Access rules
- Gravatar
- User settings

Let's look at these now.

Access rules

With the access rules, we can explicitly permit or prohibit certain usernames, email addresses, or hosts (computers) from accessing or joining our social networking site.

There are quite a few different reasons why we may wish to do this. Let's take a look at a few specific examples:

- Disposable email addresses
- Perhaps all accounts originating from a free email provider should be blocked, except for one or two individual exceptions
- We may wish to prohibit swear words from our users' usernames

Blocking email domains

To block an entire email domain such as `pookmail.com` or `hotmail.com`, we would create two rules, both with **Deny** as the access type and **E-Mail** as the **Rule type**, and then %@ followed by their respective domain names. The % character tells the rule to match anything that comes before the @ symbol.

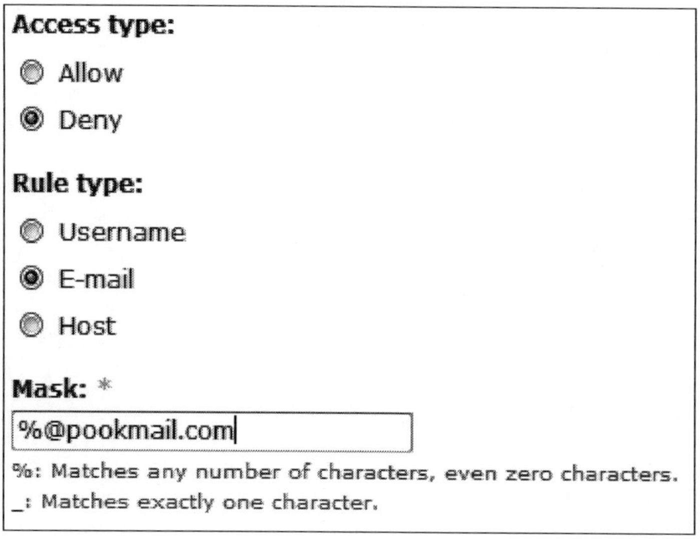

Access type:

⊙ Allow

◉ Deny

Rule type:

⊙ Username

◉ E-mail

⊙ Host

Mask: *

%@pookmail.com|

%: Matches any number of characters, even zero characters.
_: Matches exactly one character.

With an exception

If we want to block all `hotmail.com` e-mail addresses except our friend's,
`our.friend@hotmail.com`, then we would create an **allow** rule for this account.

Access type▲	Rule type	Mask	Operations	
deny	e-mail	%@pookmail.com	edit	delete
deny	e-mail	%@hotmail.com	edit	delete
allow	e-mail	our.friend@hotmail.com	edit	delete

Preventing swear words in our user's usernames

Creating rules with **Username** as the **Rule type** and the swear word (with a % on
either side) will prevent such usernames from being registered.

Checking rules

The **Check rules** link at the top of the access rules page, allows us to check these
rules by entering a username, email address, or hostname to see if that would be
permitted or prohibited on our site.

Be careful!

If you add certain "bad words" with the wildcard (%) character on both sides, you can prevent some genuine signups; so this should be used only for extreme words.

User settings

From here, we can configure the registration requirements of our users, email templates used for new accounts and so on, and users' picture settings.

User registration settings

We can determine what security precautions should be taken when a new account is registered. New accounts:

- Can only be created by an administrator
- Can be created by a visitor, but require administrator approval
- Can be created by a visitor without administrator approval and in addition to the previous two, require user email verification

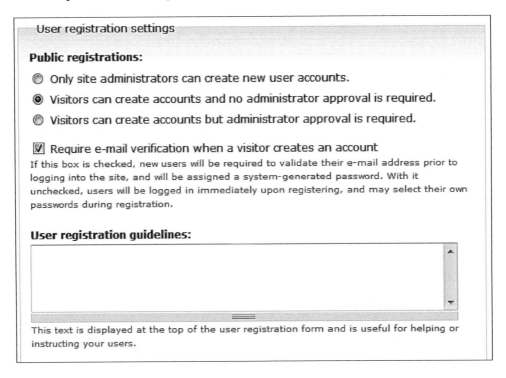

Requiring email verification is a good idea. It is the very first and most basic method to help prevent spam and abusive user accounts. The **User registration guidelines** box can be used to provide some help for our users, and perhaps a link to some legal terms and conditions to help protect ourselves from liability.

User email settings

Users will often receive an email from our site automatically when:

- We create a new account for them
- They create an account
- They create an account which is pending our approval
- They request a new password
- They need to verify their email addresses
- Their accounts have been blocked
- Their accounts have been deleted

The **User e-mail settings** area allows us to change the contents of these emails.

Click on **Administer | User management | User settings | User e-mail settings** further down the page.

User e-mail settings

Drupal sends emails whenever new users register on your site, and optionally, may also notify users after other account actions. Using a simple set of content templates, notification e-mails can be customized to fit the specific needs of your site.

▷ Welcome, new user created by administrator

▷ Welcome, no approval required

▷ Welcome, awaiting administrator approval

▷ Password recovery email

▷ Account activation email

▷ Account blocked email

▷ Account deleted email

Selecting an email allows us to change the template. Within these templates, there are tokens that are replaced with specific information when they are sent, for example, the user's username or a specific link. So it is important to ensure that these are still in the template. These variables are clearly defined when editing the template. They are all listed under the template name, each of them starting with an explanation mark, for example. `!username` for the username, `!login_uri` for the link to the log in page.

Picture settings

From here, we can either enable or disable picture support. Let's enable it.

Gravatars!

Gravatars are globally recognized avatars, (an avatar being a small picture used to represent a user when making comments or posts), and are very popular among blogs and forums, with many blogs and popular forum systems supporting gravatars. They enable users to use the same avatar across all socially-oriented sites they use, should they wish to.

We installed the gravatar module and enabled the module. To enable the integration, we need to go to the **gravatar** menu in the **User management** area and check the **Enable gravatar integration** box, and save the changes.

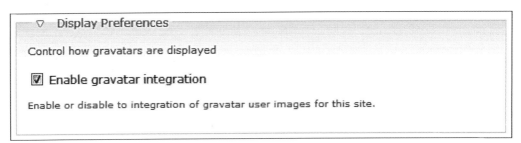

Once the integration has been enabled, the display preferences are activated, so we may configure the module (**Administer | User management | Gravatar**).

The configuration options include:

- Our preferred size of image (let's keep the default)
- Maturity filter (so we could prevent inappropriate images being displayed, very useful depending on the target audience of the site. For our site, we should be fine with the PG rating)
- Which image to use if a user does not have a gravatar

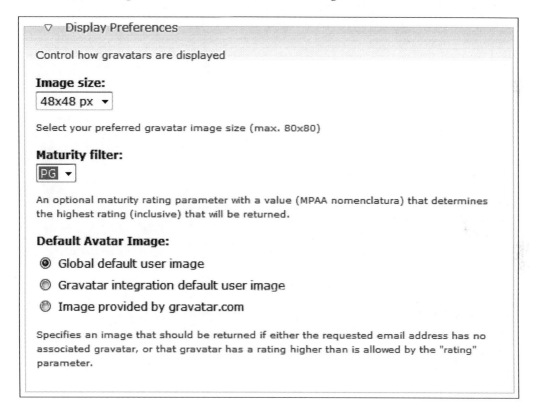

Now when a user goes to edit his/her profile, he/she are presented with an option to either upload an avatar (thanks to the **User picture** settings), or if their email address is a valid gravatar email address (that is, an email address used to sign up on the gravatar site), their gravatar will be used.

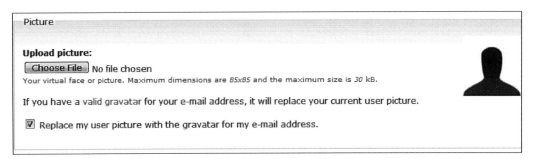

To ensure that profile pictures are displayed for our user comments and posts, we need to enable them within the theme. Click on **Administer | Site building | Themes | Global settings**. We enable **User pictures in posts** and **User pictures in comments**.

☑ User pictures in posts

☑ User pictures in comments

Now, if we have a gravatar set and we make a comment on some content on the site, our gravatar is displayed.

Comments

Great story   New   Sat, 12/06/2008 - 23:46 — Michael

Thanks for that great story!

michael

delete   edit   reply

Blog themes

While the blog theme module doesn't allow our users to create a theme of their own, it does allow them some customization of their blogs, by allowing them to select which of the installed and enabled themes they can use.

For this feature to work, we first need to enable some more themes on our site, because at the moment, we only have the default theme enabled.

Enabling themes

We will look more at themes later in the book. For now, we just need to enable some. This is done within **Site building | Themes** in the **administration** area. We simply need to check the **Enabled** checkbox next to some of the themes.

Using the blog themes module

With more than one theme available, we can now select a theme to use for our blog, from the **My account | Edit** page. In this page, there is a section entitled **Your blog theme configuration**, where we can select the theme we wish to be displayed when a user visits our blog on the site.

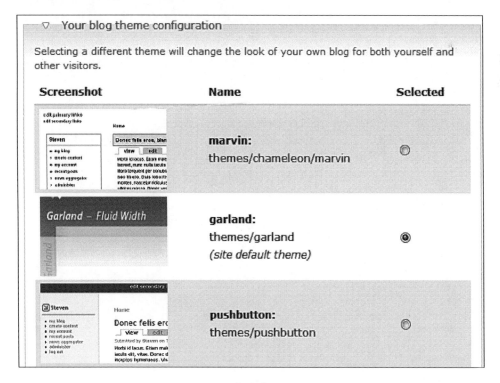

Expanding on this feature

Why not invite your users to recommend new themes to be installed and enabled?

Open ID

With the OpenID module enabled, the **User login** box is now slightly different. Beneath the standard **Username** and **Password** boxes, we have a link to **Log in using OpenID**.

If we click this link, the log in form changes to allow us to log in with our OpenID.

 Try OpenID yourself

If you don't have OpenID, and want to try it out, you can download and install a PHP based single-user standalone OpenID provider system for your own personal web site.

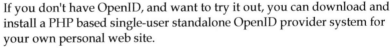
`http://siege.org/projects/phpMyID/http://siege.org/projects/phpMyID/`

Alternatively, you can sign up to an OpenID provider, such as `www.claimid.com`, which does not require you to install software on a web server.

To log in with OpenID, we just enter the web address which is our OpenID, and click **Log in**.

If this is the first time we are logging into the web site with our OpenID, then Drupal will need to create a user account for us. There are two scenarios following the first successful authentication of a user via OpenID. Either a new account is created, or we have a user already on the web site with that username, in which case, we would need to create a new account the normal way (via the registration form on the site) and then associate our OpenID with the account, if we wished so.

User already exists

When I logged in with my OpenID, I was unable to create an account because the username associated with my OpenID was Michael, which was the administrator account I had already set up. So I was presented with the following screen:

- The name *Michael* is already taken.
- OpenID registration failed for the reasons listed. You may register now, or if you already have an account you can log in now and add your OpenID under "My Account"

If this happens, our user would have to register an account with us manually, and then tie their OpenID details to their accounts, should they wish to use OpenID.

User does not exist

If the user does not already exist, then our user will be prompted to configure a new account.

Don't forget...

If you change something and can't see the log in box, simply visit the log in page directly at /user.

Summary

Our social networking web site has now expanded to enable our users to customize their experience with the site, as well as make it easier for them to use. We have also looked in more detail about managing our users, the registration process, emails which are sent to our users, and how these features tie in together.

5
Enabling User Interaction

We now have a social web site with lots of collaboration, but we still don't have a true network at this stage. We want to allow our users to build relationships with one another, as well as communicate and collaborate with one another. In this chapter, you will learn:

- How to let users build relationships with one another
- How to enable user communication
- How to enable user collaboration with groups

Dino Space: a review

So far, our users could contribute to our site using some of the user-centric modules built into Drupal. They could also extend their user profile and enhance their experience on the site.

If we looked back at Chapter 1, we would note that one of the fundamental concepts of a social networking web site was building connections with other users, which together with the connections of those users, build up a network of social links between users.

Installing the modules

Let's install all the modules we are going to use in this chapter in one go. It will save us a little time.

- User relationships (`http://drupal.org/project/user_relationships`)
- Activity (`http://drupal.org/project/activity`)
- Guestbook (`http://drupal.org/project/guestbook`)

- Organic Groups module (http://drupal.org/project/og)
- Views module (http://drupal.org/project/views)
- Notifications module (http://drupal.org/project/notifications)
- Token module (http://drupal.org/project/token)
- Messaging module (http://drupal.org/project/messaging)
- Contact module

The Activity module allows users to see a list of recent activities on the site, such as viewing profiles or topics. This module also has the functionality that can extend the User relationships module to display messages such as "User X and User Y are now friends". The Guestbook module can be configured to allow users to post comments on one another's profile pages. The Organic Groups module allows users to work together in a more social and interactive way, by segregating discussion, collaboration, and communication. The Views, Notifications, Token, and Messaging modules are all dependencies for some of the other modules and must be installed for those modules to work. Finally, the Contact module allows both site-wide and user-specific contract forms. This is a core module and simply needs to be enabled.

All these modules, apart from the Contact module, must be downloaded from the addresses shown, and extracted into the /sites/all/modules folder so that they can be installed.

Once extracted into the modules folder, we have a range of modules (The User Relationships, Activity, Organic groups, and Views modules are actually packages bringing several new modules to our installation). We need to enable the following modules:

- Activity: Activity
- Activity: Activity history
- Activity: Comment activity
- Activity: Node activity
- Activity: OG activity
- Activity: User activity
- Activity: User relationships activity
- Core optional: Contact
- Messaging: Messaging
- Notifications: Notifications
- Notifications: Content notifications
- Organic groups: Organic groups

- Organic groups: Organic groups access control
- Organic groups: Organic groups notifications
- Organic groups: Organic groups view integration
- Other: Guestbook
- Other: Token
- User Relationships: UR-API
- User Relationships: UR-Blocks
- User Relationships: UR-Defaults
- User Relationships: UR-Elaborations
- User Relationships: UR-Implications
- User Relationships: UR-Mailer
- User Relationships: UR-Node access
- User Relationships: UR-UI
- Views: Views
- Views: Views UI

With these installed, we can start to make some great improvements to our site!

Relationships

We are going to use the User Relationships module to allow our users to build relationships with one another. One of the great things about the User Relationships module is that we, the administrators can define what types of relationships are there in our site. For instance, we could have friends, family, and co-workers if we wanted. Naturally, the first stage for setting this up is planning.

Planning

Relationships with this module can either be one-way, or two-way where the relationship is reciprocal. Most social networking sites make use of friendship relationships, and this is usually a two-way relationship. Obviously, some users may wish to connect with other users who don't want to classify them as "friends". Here, we have another alternative, say "followers" to show that a user is following the contributions of another user with interest. This can be a one-way relationship. A co-workers relationship may be useful, although it would be better suited in a business-centric social network, where other relationships are set up to help define job titles and roles (for example, User A manages User B).

So, we will set up the following relationships:

- Friends
- Followers

Creating our relationships

Relationships are defined and managed within the **User management** section (**Administer | User management | Relationships**).

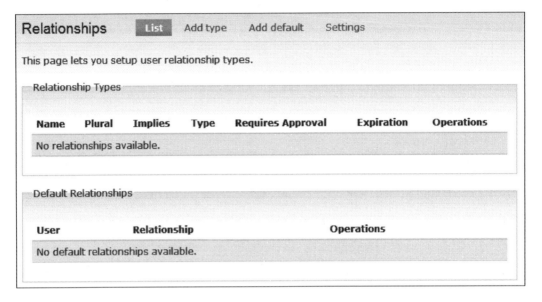

In the above screenshot, we can see the **Relationships** in our site (we currently have none!), add types of relationships, default relationships, and settings for the module. Let's click the **Add type** tab, and create our first relationship.

We need to enter a **Name** for the relationship (**Friend**) the **plural name** (**friends**), select if the "requestee" of the relationship must approve the relationship, set how long it takes for the request to expire if it is not approved, and whether it is a one-way relationship.

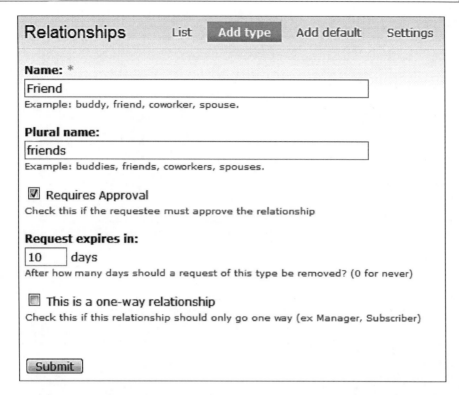

Once we click the **Submit** button, the relationship is created. We can then repeat this for the follower, except that we will not check the **requires approval** box, and we will check the **one-way relationship** box.

When creating a second relationship, we can select if the relationship implies another relationship. We don't need to select an implicit relationship for followers. However, if we were creating relationships for the dinosaurs, we could have an owner relationship, which implies that the users are automatically friends.

We can also create default relationships (via the **Add default** tab). This allows all users to have a relationship with certain users automatically, for instance, we could configure it so that all users are automatically our friends, simply by entering our username in the **Username** box, and **Friend** in the **Relationship** box.

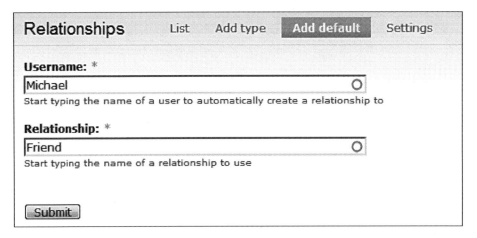

Our relationships are now set up as shown below:

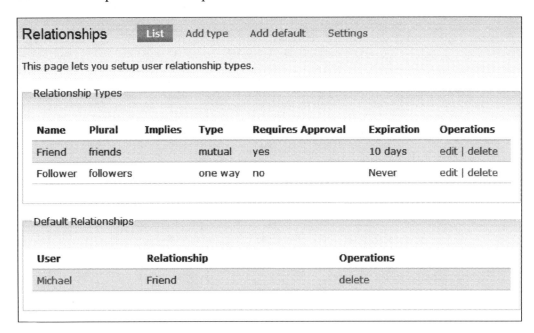

Let's now take a look at the settings for this module.

Settings

The **Settings** tab for this module allows us to configure some general settings for the module, email notifications for the module, elaborations and messages for the module.

General settings

The **General** settings allow us to set whether:

- Multiple relationships should be allowed (yes, by default)
- Links to create relationships with users should be shown on their profile page (yes by default)
- Their picture should be shown in the relationship pages (no by default)
- Users can auto approve certain relationship requests (no by default), and how many relationships should be shown per page

Enabling pictures in **relationship pages** allow users to see at a glance who their friends are. Auto approval allows users to be automatically friends with anyone who makes the request, saving them time if they are happy to do so. By extending the number of relationships per page, they don't need to move between pages so much. Now, let's make these changes.

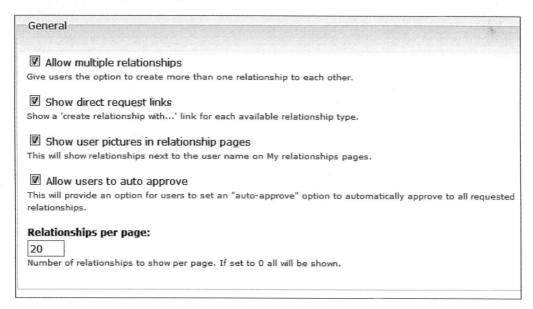

Email notifications

The **Email options** allow us to set if users can turn off the relationship messages (let's enable this; if a user gets lots of requests, it could get irritating to receive so many emails, so it is best to let them decide), and also allow us to define the content of the emails, simply by selecting the email and changing the content. A list of tokens which are substituted with values such as the username and the site's name are displayed when editing an email.

Email Options

☑ **Allow users to turn off relationship messages**
If you check this, users will have a new setting on their account edit page.

▷ Request

▷ Cancel

▷ Approve

▷ Disapprove

▷ Remove

Elaborations

The module includes an elaboration UI which allows users to send a message with their relationship request to other users. This is enabled by default, and can be disabled by checking the box.

Messages

Finally, we can manage the messages that users are presented with, when they perform certain actions.

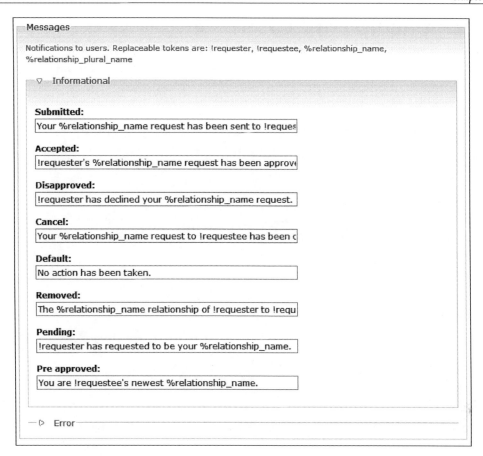

Permissions

In order for our users to create and maintain relationships with one another, we need to enable the appropriate permissions for their roles, including **can have relationships**, **maintain own relationships**, and **view user relationships**. Permissions are accessed via **Administer | User management | Permissions**.

user_relationships_api module		
can have relationships	☐	☑
user_relationships_ui module		
administer user relationships	☐	☐
maintain own relationships	☐	☑
view user relationships	☐	☑

Relationships in action

We have planned set up and configured user relationships into our site, and set the necessary permissions to enable our users to build and maintain relationships. Now, let us see them in action!

Default relationship

If we create a new user on our site (**Administer | User management | Users**) to experiment with, we should find that by visiting their profile, we are already their friend, as we set up a default relationship for all users to be friends with us.

Creating a relationship with another user

If we create another user, log in as this user, and then visit the profile of the user we created in the previous section, we have options to become both the user's friend as well as follower.

When we click the link to become a user's friend, we are prompted to provide an **Elaboration** (a message explaining how we met, or how we know each other), and confirm that we wish to **Send** the request.

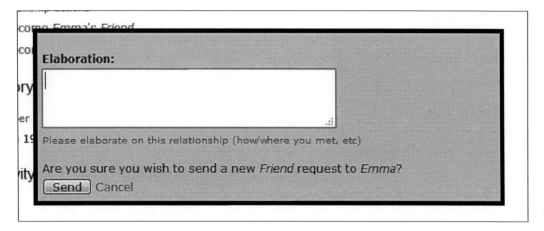

Now, on this user's profile, we see that we have a pending friend request with this user.

If we now log in as the user we requested to be friends with, we can see on that user's account page, there is a message informing them of the friend request, which can be approved from their **pending relationship requests**.

Michael2 has requested to be your *Friend*. Please view your pending relationship requests to approve them.

My relationships

The **My relationships** page (accessed via the **My relationships** link in the main menu) shows us all our relationships, any pending relationships, and allows us to see relationships filtered based on type.

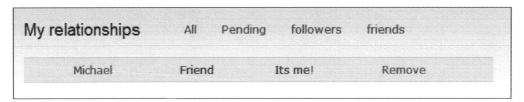

If we click the **Pending** tab, we can see the relationship request we've just created, and we can either **Approve** or **Disapprove** this request.

If we click **Approve**, we are presented with an elaboration form to explain the relationship, which also requires us to confirm a final time before the relationship is approved.

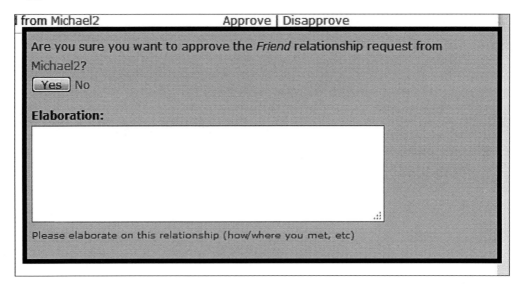

User activities

The activity module logs and displays user activities such as profile views, topic views, and so on, and can be viewed as a public activity log showing activity for all users on the site recently or by the relationship type so we can filter the list to show the activity of users we have established a relationship with.

Permissions

For our users to use this feature, we must give them permission to view own activity and view public activity via the **Permission** section (**Administer | User management | Permissions**).

Permission	anonymous user	authenticated user
activity module		
administer activity	☐	☐
view own activity	☐	☑
view public activity	☐	☑

With these permissions granted, they can see a list of activities for all users on the site, as well as their own activity.

Activities in action

To view the activities module in action, we simply need to click the **Activity** link in the main menu. Clicking the link takes us to the public activity list, which can then be filtered down based on relationships that we have established on the site.

Public list

The public list shows the activities for all users on the site.

Activity			
All activity	My activity	My friends' activity	My followers' activity

Date	Message
01/06/2009 - 00:28	Michael logged in to Dino Space!
01/06/2009 - 00:28	Michael logged off of Dino Space!
01/06/2009 - 00:25	Michael logged in to Dino Space!
01/06/2009 - 00:25	Emma logged off of Dino Space!
01/06/2009 - 00:25	Emma logged in to Dino Space!

At this stage, it is not reporting relationship status changes (we will address this shortly), but includes login, logout, profile views, and so on.

Friends list

We can filter the list to see only the activity of the users we have relationships with, bringing Facebook-style feeds to our site.

Activity			
All activity	My activity	**My friends' activity**	My followers' activity

Date	Message
01/06/2009 - 00:25	Emma logged off of Dino Space!
01/06/2009 - 00:25	Emma logged in to Dino Space!
01/06/2009 - 00:14	Emma logged off of Dino Space!
01/06/2009 - 00:14	Emma logged off of Dino Space!
01/06/2009 - 00:14	Emma logged off of Dino Space!
01/06/2009 - 00:13	Emma logged in to Dino Space!
01/06/2009 - 00:13	Emma logged off of Dino Space!

We can also view our own activity, should we wish so.

Settings

With a feature which reveals such detailed information about our users' usage of the site, it is important that we give them the option to opt out of having their activity logged. This can be done via **Administer | Site configuration | Activity Settings**.

We should check the **Allow user privacy opt-out** box to ensure that our users can opt out of the feature, and maintain a higher level of privacy when using our site.

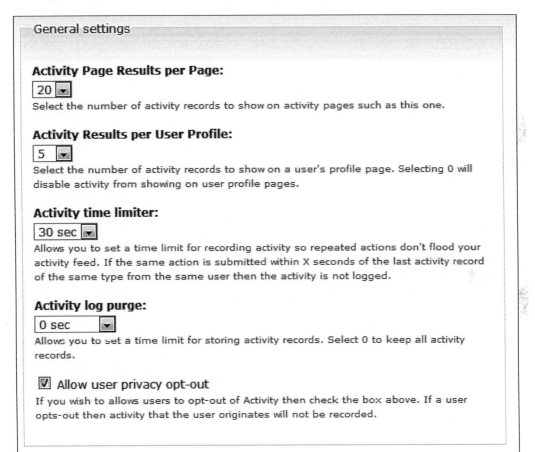

We can also change the text which is shown for each activity, including those provided by the User Relationships module, via the **User relationships activity settings page** link.

> **Activity contrib modules**
>
> Click on the links below to configure the activity settings for the activity contrib modules you have installed.
>
> Comment activity settings page
>
> Node activity settings page
>
> User activity settings page
>
> User relationships activity settings page

The activities module supports displaying notifications for relationship changes. However, despite being enabled by default, it does not initially display relationship change notifications. This is corrected by changing the settings (**Administer | Site configuration | Activities | User Relationships Module Activity Settings page**) and then saving the settings. The activity module then displays relationship notifications too.

01/06/2009 - 00:32	Michael viewed Emma's profile
01/06/2009 - 00:32	Michael is now followers with Emma
01/06/2009 - 00:32	Michael viewed Emma's profile

The settings on that configuration page allow us to define which relationships (**Token types**) have their activities recorded, and for which **Operation types** (for example, approving a friend request). We can also change the messages that are displayed.

If we visit our profile page, and then click the **edit** link, we also have the option to opt out of having our activity recorded in the activity module.

> ▽ **Activity privacy settings**
>
> ☐ Do not record my site activity
> If you wish keep your site activity from appearing in the activity pages, check the box.

All our users have to do is check this box, and save their profile to opt out. It may be worth detailing in the site's terms and conditions that their activities are recorded and publicly displayed unless they opt out.

Profile comments with the Guestbook module

The Guestbook module provides two very useful features:

- A site-wide guestbook
- Individual user guestbooks

This allows us to either have a site-wide guestbook or a guestbook for each user, enabling profile messages to be posted (as with many social networks). Alternatively, we can have both these features enabled. A site-wide guestbook would allow us to collect feedback, testimonials and comments from our users in a simple way. So we would want to have it enabled too.

Settings

First, let's take a look at the settings for this module, and ensure we have it set up in a way we are happy with. The module is configured via **Administer | Site configuration | Guestbook**.

The first group of settings defines which mode the module is running in. By default, it is set to enable both site-wide and per-user guestbooks. As this is the setup we want, let's leave this as it is.

Mode:
- ◉ Site and user guestbooks
- ◎ Site guestbook only
- ◎ User guestbooks only

Next, we can configure the site-wide guestbook by setting a title and introduction text for it, as well as an email address to send notifications of new entries to. Let's customize this to make the user feel more welcome, and set a notification email address to inform us of the new entries.

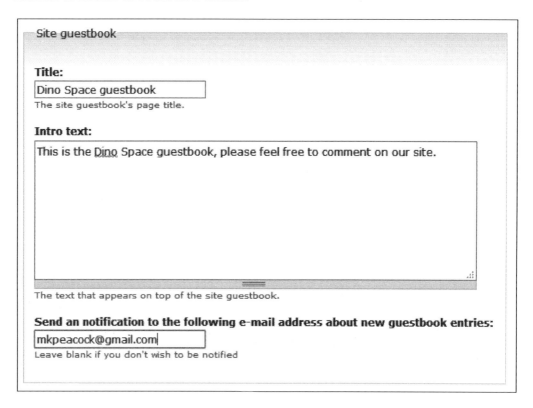

Next, we have settings for **User guestbooks**, which defines whether a link to the users shown in the guestbooks page (which we will look at shortly) should take us to their profile page or to their guestbook page. Let's select the **User guestbook** option so that users can comment on one another's profiles without having to view their profiles, and then click the **guestbook** links.

User guestbooks

Users can individually disable their guestbook or add an intro text on the user account page.

User link to profile or guestbook:

○ User profile

◉ User guestbook

When displaying a user should the link show the user profile or the user guestbook?

Next, we have display options, which allow us to control how guestbooks are displayed–the number of entries shown on a page, which information is shown on the entry, and where the links for navigating between pages is displayed.

Display options

Entries per page:

20

The number of guestbook entries per page.

Toggle display:

☑ Submission date

☑ Anonymous poster e-mail

☑ Anonymous poster website

☑ Comments

Position of pager:

○ Above the entries

◉ Below the entries

○ Above and below the entries

Finally, we have the post settings, so we can control how the text submitted is filtered, any additional fields which we should request from users who are not logged-in, and where the entry submission form is located.

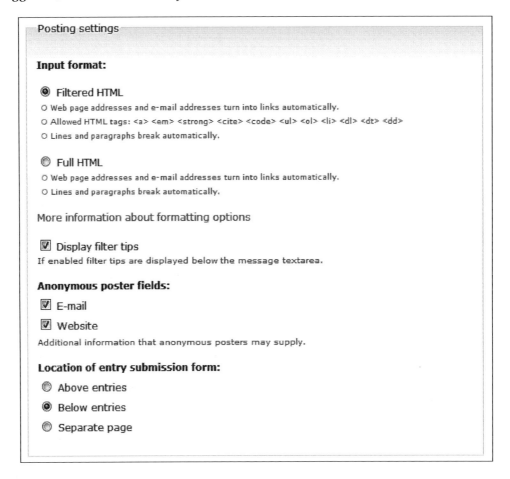

Having the entry submission form below the guestbook entries puts a greater focus on the existing content, although it is really a personal call based on our preferences as the site administrator.

Permissions

To allow our users to view the guestbooks and post guestbook entries, we need to grant them the following permissions: **access site guestbook**, **access user guestbooks**, **post in site guestbook** and **post in user guestbooks**. We should also allow users who are not logged-in (anonymous users) to **access site guestbook** and **access user guestbooks**.

guestbook module		
access site guestbook	☑	☑
access user guestbooks	☑	☑
administer all guestbooks	☐	☐
post in site guestbook	☐	☑
post in user guestbooks	☐	☑

Site-wide guestbook

If we click the **Site guestbook** link on the main menu (don't forget that, menu links can be changed from the **Administration** options), we are shown the site-wide guestbook.

Dino Space guestbook

This is the Dino Space guestbook, please feel free to comment on our site.

Michael

Really like the site!   Tue, 01/06/2009 - 12:21

» Delete entry | Add comment

Add guestbook entry

Message: *

```



```

O Web page addresses and e-mail addresses turn into links automatically.
O Allowed HTML tags: <a> <em> <strong> <cite> <code> <ul> <ol> <li> <dl> <dt> <dd>
O Lines and paragraphs break automatically.

[Send]

Here, users can post any comments they wish to, or comment on existing comments building discussion.

User guestbooks

Most importantly, we can now see per-user guestbooks, by viewing a user's profile. The guestbook works in the same way as the site-wide guestbook, except that it is tied to the users' own profiles, and the users can also change some settings for their own guestbook.

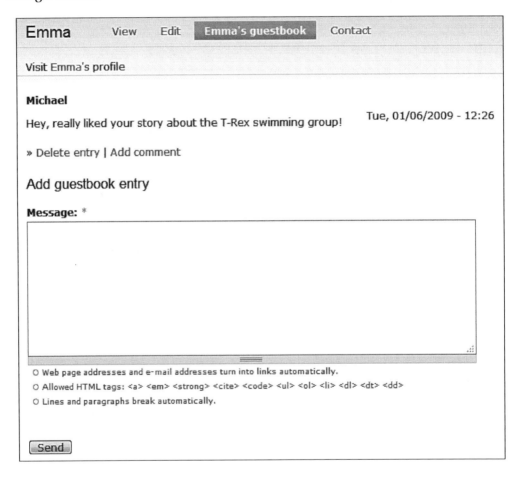

Viewing guestbooks

In the main navigation menu, the **Guestbooks** link in the menu let's see quickly which user guestbooks have recently been commented on, how many entries they have, and when was the last time the site-wide guestbook had a new entry posted.

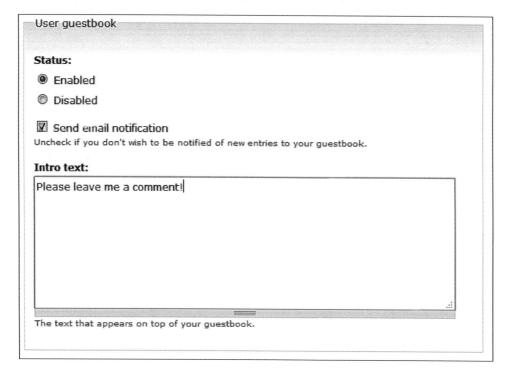

Guestbooks

Dino Space guestbook (1 entry, last update: 6 min)

User guestbooks

user	entries	last update ▼
Emma	1 entry	1 min
Michael	0 entries	never
MichaelP	0 entries	never
Michael2	0 entries	never

Clicking one of the usernames in the list takes us directly to that user's guestbook page. This is what we set earlier as the location we will be taken to when we click on a username in the guestbook list, as opposed to taking us to the users main profile page.

When a user goes to edit their account or their profile, they also have the ability to enable or disable their guestbook, set their own introduction text to the guestbook, and set if they wish to be notified of new entries via email.

User guestbook

Status:

◉ Enabled

○ Disabled

☑ Send email notification
Uncheck if you don't wish to be notified of new entries to your guestbook.

Intro text:

Please leave me a comment!

The text that appears on top of your guestbook.

Now, we have a social network where users can comment on one another's profiles, and these comments can be seen by the rest of the site.

Contacting users

The contact module provides two new features to our site:

- A site contact form: This enables users of the site to privately get in touch with us — the site administrators.
- User contact forms: Allowing users to privately contact one another directly.

We obviously would want to make use of both of these, a site-wide form so that we can be contacted with web site-related issues, and user forms so that our users can privately communicate with one another.

User contact forms

Since the module is enabled, we now have user contact forms already available with us. All we need to do is visit a user's profile and click the **Contact** tab shown on their profile.

This contact form allows a user to email another user, but keeps the recipients' email address private, unless they chose to reply. From here, we can enter a subject for the message, the message itself, and check a box to request a copy of the email to be sent to our own email address as well for our reference.

From:
Michael <michael@dinospace.net>

To:
Emma

Subject: *
Teething trouble

Message: *

Hey there!

I read one of your posts a while back where you mentioned your T-Rex was having teething problems. My T-Rex has just started to get teeth, and was wondering what you used to help them through it,

Many thanks,

Michael

☑ Send yourself a copy.

Send e-mail

Clicking **Send e-mail** then sends the email, without any confirmations.

Site-wide contact form

The site-wide contact form enables our users to get in touch with us—the site administrator, or someone else who is assisting with the running of the site. When a user completes the contact form, they must select a category that their enquiry is relating to. We can then route the email to a different person depending on the category selected.

To configure the module correctly, we need to:

- Create a number of categories for the contact form, and set up the email addresses which they should route to
- Add information to the top of the page
- Enable the contact forms menu item

Creating the contact form categories

First, let's think about what we will use our contact form for.

- Gathering feedback on the web site
- Resolving member disputes
- Dealing with copyright content posted on the site
- Dealing with technical support issues relating to the web site

Feedback and copyright content issues are issues which we may wish to deal with ourselves, whereas member disputes and technical support issues could be handled by other members of our community who are happy to help out.

The contact module configuration options are in **Administer | Site building | Contact form**.

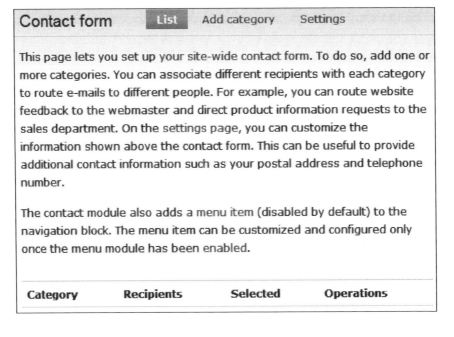

This page provides detailed instructions on how the module works and how it can be configured. It also lists the various categories related to the form and the email addresses it sends **Contact form** submissions to. Different categories can be set up to send the submissions to different email addresses. Currently, there are no "routes" listed on this page. We need to click the **Add category** link at the top to add our routes.

Here, we enter details for:

- The **Category (website feedback)** which the user will select from a drop-down list when the contact form is displayed
- The **Recipients** (webmaster@dinospace.net) the email address inquiries of this type should be sent to
- An **Auto-Reply** if we wish to automatically send the user an email, for instance, to thank them for their feedback
- A **Weight** to determine the order of this option in the drop-down list
- If this option should be **Selected** as the default option in the drop-down list

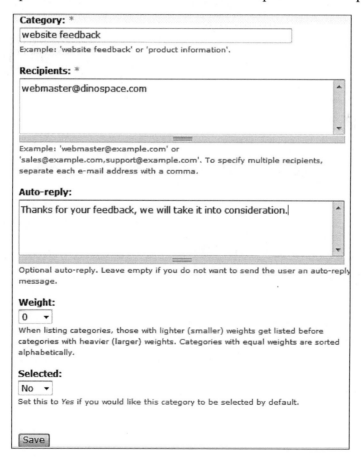

So, for the users we have for our contact form, we would need to create the following routes:

Gathering user feedback

- Category: website feedback
- Recipients: webmaster@dinospace.net
- Auto-reply: Thanks for your feedback, we will take it into consideration
- Weight: 0
- Selected: No

Dealing with member disputes

- Category: member disputes
- Recipients: moderator@dinospace.net, webmaster@dinospace.net
- Auto-reply: Your message has been received; we will look into this matter as soon as possible
- Weight: 1
- Selected: No

Dealing with copyright content reports

- Category: report copyrighted content
- Recipients: webmaster@dinospace.net
- Auto-reply: Your report has been received and will be investigated
- Weight: 2
- Selected: No

Providing technical support to our users

- Category: technical support
- Recipients: moderator@dinospace.net
- Auto-reply: Thanks for your message, we will get back to you as soon as we can
- Weight: 3
- Selected: Yes

Adding information to the top of the form

The **Settings** tab allows us to provide a description for the Contact **form**, as well as the option to set an hourly threshold to prevent users from abusing the **Contact form**, and the option to disable the per-user contact forms.

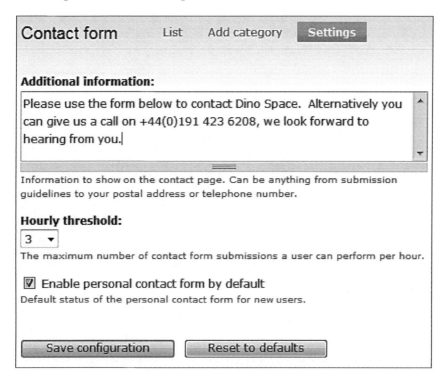

Let's enter a brief description for our **Contact form** and then click **Save configuration** to save the changes.

Enabling the contact form in the menu

With the **Contact form** setup and ready to be used, we just need to enable the link in the menu, so that our users can easily reach it and use it. The menu link can be enabled from **Administer | Site building | Menus**. From here, we go into the **Navigation** menu and check the enabled box for the **Contact form** module.

Once enabled, we then need to click **Save configuration** at the bottom of the page to save the changes made.

Taking the content form for a spin

We now have a new contact link in our menu, which takes our users to the new contact form.

The site-wide contact form is very similar to the per-user contact form, but with a few key differences:

- The information we entered is displayed above the contact form
- The name of whom we are sending the message to is not there
- We have a drop-down list of categories

If we click on the **Send e-mail** button with **website feedback** selected from the categories list, an email would be sent to webmaster@dinospace.net as we have configured it to. However, as we are working from a local installation, it won't be able to send the message.

Groups

Groups, courtesy—the Organic groups module, can enhance our community by providing an area for groups of users to communicate and work together. Users can create groups, join groups, contribute to groups, and subscribe to groups, thus creating a series of smaller communities within the site.

Groups for Dino Space

Why might we want to provide groups in our Dino Space network? Let's take a look at some potential groups:

- T-Rex owners groups
- New users group—help and support for using the site
- UK Dinosaur owners group—related discussion and comments specific to the dinosaur owners residing in the UK

Groups support a number of different membership options, including:

- Open membership—where requests for memberships are automatically approved
- Moderated—where new requests must be approved
- Invite only—new members can only join on invitation by an administrator
- Closed—all memberships are managed only by an administrator

This allows us to have private groups should we wish that option.

Of course, as these are Organic groups, users can create new groups as the need for them arises.

Organic Groups module

The Organic groups module requires some simple configuration. To get it up and running, we need to:

- Create a new content type to act as the root node for a group
- Configure group settings

- Configure the page content type to allow it to be contributed to a group
- Configure the relevant blocks

Create group content type

We need to create a new content type from the **Administer | Content management | Content types** section, by clicking the **Add content type** tab at the top of the page.

Under the **Identification** tab, let's call it a **Group** and the type **group**.

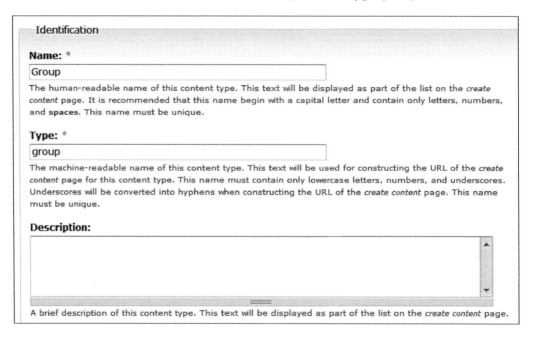

Next, under the **Organic groups** section, we need to select this content type as a **Group node**, so that creating the content of this type effectively creates a new group for us.

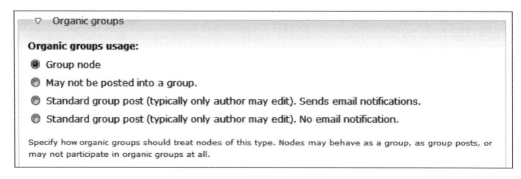

Next, we click **Save content type** to save the new content type.

Configure page content type

So, we have a content type which can be used as a group. That is great! But we need to be able to post information into the group, preferably by creating pages within the group. To do this, we need to configure the page content type, to allow it to be posted into a group.

From **Administer | Content management | Content types**, we need to click the **edit** link associated with the **Page** content type. Under the **Organic groups** section, we need to set the content type to be a **Standard group post**, which allows it to be posted within a group.

Enabling the block

The Organic groups module comes with a number of blocks which can be displayed at the side of our Drupal site to provide further information about the current group, and groups within our site generally. To configure the block, we need to navigate to **Administer | Site building | Blocks**.

The following blocks should be set to **Right sidebar**:

- **Group notifications**
- **Group details**
- **New groups**

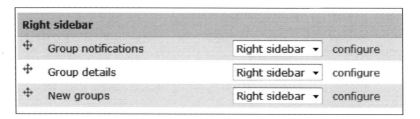

The **New groups** block provides a list of recently created groups in our Drupal site. The **Group details** and **Group notifications** blocks are only displayed when they are within a group.

Creating a group

To create a new group, we must create some new content, of type group from **Create content | group**.

Let's create a T-Rex owners group. We will call it **T-Rex Owners**, with a **Description** of, **a group of owners of T-Rex Dinosaurs**, and a **Mission statement** detailing the group.

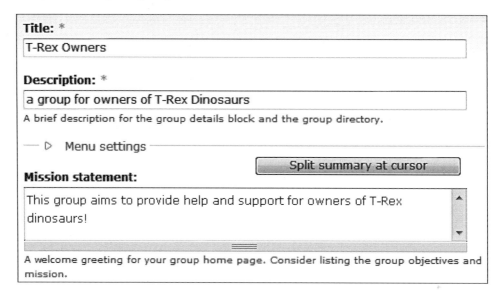

Let's set this up to be an open group, so that anyone can join instantly. Let's place an option for joining the group on the user registration page, as well as make it available in the directory of groups.

Membership requests: *

◉ Open - membership requests are accepted immediately.

◎ Moderated - membership requests must be approved.

◎ Invite only - membership must be created by an administrator.

◎ Closed - membership is exclusively managed by an administrator.

How should membership requests be handled in this group? When you select *closed*, users will not be able to join **or** leave.

☑ Registration form

May users join this group during registration? If checked, a corresponding checkbox will be added to the registration form.

☑ List in groups directory

Should this group appear on the list of groups page? Disabled if the group is set to *private group*.

Using our group

Once our group is created, we are taken to it. Let's review the group screen.

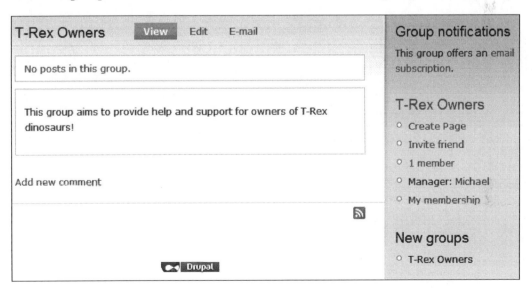

From here we can:

- See that there are no posts in the group at the moment
- See the mission statement
- Add a new comment
- Edit the group
- Email subscribers of this group
- Set if we wish to receive an email every time a new message is posted to the group using the **Group notifications** block.
- Create a page, invite a friend to the group, see members of the group, see the manager of the group, and manage our membership of the group from the **Group details** block.
- See new groups added to the site, from the **New groups** block.

This module opens up a whole new world with our site, allowing us to create subcommunities to discuss and collaborate on various topics. We could create groups for discussing site policy and direction, and create a group for users who are contributing, using the book module. Groups can give these users private areas to thrash out ideas, or public areas where anyone can participate, while maintaining a list of users who are following or contributing to the group.

Summary

We have taken our site with collaboration features, and added a wealth of communication features including the ability for users to create networks of users, allowing users to help promote the site, and communicate with one another using the contact module. We have also provided additional communication and collaboration tools with the Organic groups module, helping to bring a more community-based environment to our site.

Communicating with our Users

6

Our users can communicate with one another, which is great, but quite often as an administrator the need may arise for us to communicate with a user or users on our site. It may be to remind them about the web site or to inform active users about new changes to the site, which they may not have been made aware of.

In this chapter, you will learn:

- About mailing lists, and how to use them with our Drupal social network
- How to use an offline approach for contacting our users
- How to use blocks of content to get a message across to your users

Getting started

We are going to look at a few different modules, some of which we will use. These need to be installed first, so let's do that now to save us time.

The modules

We need to download the following modules:

- Addresses module (`http://drupal.org/project/addresses`) enable the **Addresses**, **Addresses - Phone/Fax** and **Addresses - Users** components.
- Simplenews module (`http://drupal.org/project/simplenews`)

And extract them to our `sites/all/modules` folder, and enable them via the administration interface.

A look back

We have already looked at one very important aspect to communicate with our users—**user e-mail settings**. Within the User settings page (**Administer | User management | User settings**), we have a group of settings under the heading User e-mail settings. These are various email templates that are sent to our users upon certain events, such as registration, account activation, password reset, account being blocked or account being deleted. The content of these emails can be very important depending on the nature of the web site. In our Dino Space site, we may use a very informal, welcoming and fun tone for our automated emails. But for a business-oriented social network, we would want to use a much more formal tone.

Modules

Don't forget, many modules also have their own email templates for sending emails to users, all of which can normally be changed easily from their respective sections in the administration area.

Communicating on an individual basis

As we have installed the contact form module on our site, we can also communicate with our users on an individual basis using the contact forms on their profiles. This is handy for those times when we do need to contact an individual user, maybe because of complaints against them by other members of the community, or perhaps to invite them to become a moderator or contributor to the site.

Alternatively, we can contact the user directly via their email addresses listed in their accounts, as this is viewable from the administration area.

Inactive users

We may wish to contact users who have not been active on the site for a long time, to remind them that the site is still there, and that they would be welcome to become active in the community once again. Drupal records the time a user was last active, which allows us to easily sort the list of users by their activity.

A module (Inactive user) is available for Drupal 5, which is intended to contact inactive users automatically, but (at the time of writing this) one is not available for Drupal 6. You may wish to keep watch on the modules list on the Drupal.org web site to see if anything comes up in future `http://drupal.org/project/inactive_user`.

Communicating with individuals publicly

Don't forget, we also have access to all of the communication methods available for our users to communicate with one another, such as replying to posts, commenting on content, or posting on their profiles. So if we need to contact a user, and we can contact them publicly, we can use these features.

Mailing lists

Drupal has a number of modules available for sending emails to our users. Many of them are still currently under heavy development, or had their development stopped after the release of a previous version of Drupal. One of these modules is Simplenews, which is a native Drupal system for managing newsletters.

One limitation of the Simplenews module, and most of the modules available, is that it can't send to all our users; it requires users to subscribe to the mailing list.

We can manage the Simplenews module via **Administer | Newsletter**. The features available to us are quite comprehensive. Let's have a look at how the module works:

- **Newsletters** are created and managed from here
- Users subscribe to various **Newsletters**
- Users can be imported into **Newsletters** to become a subscriber
- A message is sent to a newsletter (this is referred to as an issue) by creating **Newsletter** content
- Issues which have been sent are saved within the module
- Issues which have not yet been sent are saved within the module as drafts

By default, we have a **newsletter**, which is generic to our site based on our site name.

From here we can also create new **Newsletters** should we wish so. The **Subscriptions** tab allows us to see and manage the subscriptions to our various newsletters, the **Sent issues** tab lists issues sent out to the **newsletter** lists, and the **Drafts** tab lists issues which are still being written. From within the **Settings** tab, we can set how new issues for **newsletters** are created, as well as the email address shown as the sender of issues.

 Don't forget to set the permissions; you want your users to be able to subscribe to **newsletters**.

Users can subscribe to **newsletters** from within their account, or we can enable blocks for the relevant newsletters we have on our site.

To send an "issue" to our newsletter list, we need to create the issue as a new content element via **Create content | Newsletter issue**.

We enter the subject of our email as the **Title**, select the newsletter to send the message to from the **Newsletter** drop-down list, and the message is entered into the **Body** box.

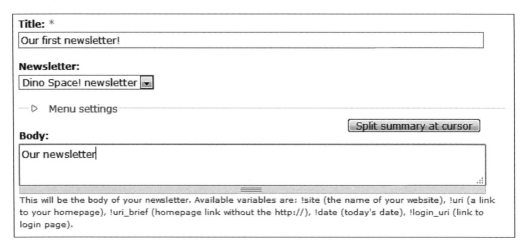

Beneath these options, we have some newsletter specific-options within the **Newsletter sending options** box. These options allow us to set the **priority** of the email message (this is often ignored by email clients), if we wish to request a receipt to see if a user has read the message (this is also often ignored by email clients) and finally, we can select a **sending** method.

There are three sending methods, which are:

- **Don't send now** — this won't send the message, and will save it as a draft.
- **Send one test newsletter to the test address** — this will send the email message to the test email addresses, which we can set in the administration area. This allows us to review the newsletter, as if we were a subscriber, make any final alterations and then send it to our list.
- **Send newsletter** — this sends the email to our newsletter list.

How to send an email to all our users?

We can use the module to send an email to all of our users, by taking advantage of the subscriber import feature. Within **Administer | Content management | Newsletters | Subscriptions**, we have the ability to **Import subscriptions**, as shown in the following screenshot:

Importing subscribers consists of entering the **E-mail addresses** (separated by a comma) and selecting the **newsletter** which we wish the user to subscribe to. To get all of our current members to subscribe to the mailing list, we could export all of our users' email addresses directly from the Drupal database, using a tool such as phpMyAdmin. If we use the tool correctly, we can even get the data in a comma-separated list ready to be pasted into the form.

HTML emails

In order to send HTML (that is, nicely formatted) emails, and emails as attachments to our newsletters, we would need to install the Mime Mail module from (`http://drupal.org/project/mimemail`).

Give it a try

We have covered module installation and configuration extensively; so why not try and install the module yourself and experiment with HTML newsletters.

Legalities

There are legalities involved with sending bulk emails, and mailing lists, especially with regards to SPAM. Most countries have their own laws relating to this. More information on the legalities of sending bulk mailings is available in Chapter 10, *Promoting your Site*.

Throttling

When web sites send out bulk email campaigns, it is important to be careful about their frequency of emails. If all emails in the campaign are sent at once, this could be seen as a sign of SPAM, leading to blacklisting on mail servers, and also penalties from many shared hosts. If emails are sent out slowly, it may take a long time for a campaign to be sent out to all recipients.

The Simplenews module allows us to configure the frequency of the emails sent. These settings can be accessed from **Administer | Site configuration | Simplenews | Send mail**. Here the cron box is checked, indicating that emails are sent each time the Drupal cron script is called. The **Cron throttle** defines how many newsletters are sent each time the Drupal cron script is called. By default, it is set to 20, which is very low. So this should be changed perhaps to 100 or 500. You may wish to contact your hosting company for advice on email limits imposed by them.

Third-Party Services

Besides allowing us to run our own email newsletter service from within Drupal, a number of the available modules allow us to make use of third-party mailing list systems.

PHPList

PHPList is a popular mailing list system written in PHP, if we were to use this system (particularly useful if our Drupal social network is part of a group of sites, or part of a larger site which does not use Drupal), we can use the PHPList integration module to:

- Synchronize users from Drupal to our PHPList system
- Send targeted mailings based on the values of a users profile
- Allow users to manage their PHPList subscriptions from within their account
- Bulk import into PHPList, if we already have a Drupal installation running with many users

This module can be downloaded from `http://drupal.org/project/phplist`, while PHPList can be downloaded from `http://www.phplist.com/`

 PHPList involves some server configuration; so if PHPList is the solution for you, make sure you read the documentation thoroughly.

Constant contact

Constant contact (`http://www.constantcontact.com/index.jsp`) is an online email marketing service, which manages newsletter subscriptions itself, with a particular focus on privacy and security for subscribers on mailing lists. Drupal 5 had a module to easily link into a constant contact account, `http://drupal.org/project/constant_contact`. This module, at the time of writing is not available for Drupal 6. But it is worth looking out for updates of this module or an alternative module to take its place if you wish to use constant contact to provide newsletters for your social network.

Google Groups

Google Groups are essentially mini social networks that operate in a way similar to groups in our network with the Organic Groups module. Many organizations and projects, such as open source software projects, make use of Google Groups to complement their communication and collaboration areas. If you wish to use Google Groups to complement your social network, then there is a module to allow users to subscribe to your group directly from the site. The module can be downloaded from `http://drupal.org/project/google_groups`. This module would probably be of little use if you used the organic groups module because the organic groups module provides very similar functionality. Problems with using a service such as Google Groups is that we are limited in terms of controlling the layout of our communications losing any branding associated with our site, and a potential loss of revenue when we may have used advertisements on our site or on our own newsletter.

Direct contact

If our social network is an extension of something else, for instance an online supplement to an organization dedicated to the promotion and support of keeping dinosaurs as pets, then we may wish to contact users of our social network using an offline method.

The Address module allows users to supply a physical address and a telephone number, which means we could post newsletters to our users. This would primarily be of use to organizations which are already producing paper mailers to a wide audience, where the online social network is used to complement the services provided by these organizations; otherwise offline contacting may not be cost effective.

The address module

Having installed the address module, and having given users permissions to create an address book, we can collect the addresses, telephone numbers, and fax numbers of our users.

Users perspective

From the users perspective, they can easily store and edit addresses and contact details from within their accounts, via the **Address Book** tab.

My account	View	Edit	Address Book

Click here to add a new address.

address	options
Office (default) Suite 57, Design Works William Street Newcastle, United Kingdom NE10 0JP	edit / delete

Administrators perspective

Unfortunately, this module was designed to complement other modules (for example, the e-Commerce module) in providing a convenient location for users to store their address for later use (such as ordering products for delivery with the e-Commerce module). There is no back-end interface to allow us, as administrators, to view the contact details of our users. We can, however, gain access to the information from the database directly, and can then maintain our own records from there, or from the $user array via custom PHP code. An alternative would be to create additional user profile fields, which can be read only by administrators.

Content blocks

Modules and themes often make use of blocks to display small blocks of content in specific areas of the web site, generally including the web sites header, the sidebars on the left and righthand side of the screen, the footer, and the main content area, as well as dynamic functionality, such as group information in the Organic groups module. Blocks we have previously been using, such as with the Organic groups module, are dynamic and populated by the modules that created them. Blocks don't have to be dynamic; we can create blocks of our own to display content that doesn't change dynamically.

We can make use of these blocks to display information and messages to our users. For instance, if we wanted to communicate with guest users, we could create a content block with information on the benefits of joining the site.

Creating a content block for anonymous users

1. Navigate to **Administer | Site building | Blocks**.

2. Select the **Add block** tab.

3. Enter a **Description**, **Title** and **Body** for the block, with the benefits of joining in the **Block body** box.

4. Under **Role-specific visibility** settings, select **Show blog** for specific roles for anonymous users.

5. Under **Page-specific visibility** settings, select the block to be visible on all pages.

6. **Save** block.

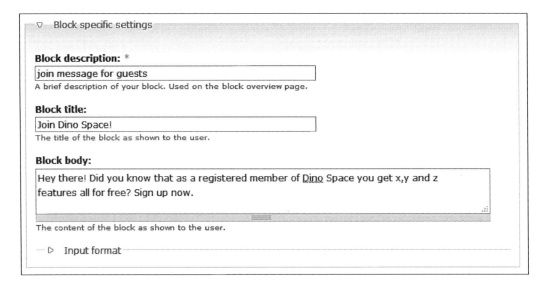

Once created, the block is displayed on our site for users who are not logged in:

Theme customizations for communication

We could also use the look and feel of our site to communicate with our users. The following are some examples of what we could do:

- A simple bar of information, perhaps relating to a specific feature
- Pop-up windows (although considered a bad design practice)
- **CSS (cascading style sheets)** pop ups with information
- A collapsible message, where the user can click an icon to expand an administrative message, which we can update periodically

These options require knowledge of HTML, CSS, and Drupal themes.

Summary

In this chapter, we looked at how we—as administrators can communicate with our users using a variety of methods including:

- Features that we have previously covered in other chapters
- Newsletters and mailing lists
- Third-party mailing lists
- Content blocks

We now have a fully functional social network. Our users can contribute to the site, communicate with each other, and we can communicate with them. In the next chapter, we will look at how easy it is to create custom modules to fit the needs of almost any site by creating a custom module of our very own.

7
Improving our Network with Custom Modules

Throughout this book we have seen how flexible Drupal is because of its modular structure, and how we can easily extend the functionality of the web site to fit our needs. Previously, we have made use of the existing modules to add functionality. In this chapter, we will look into the modular system in more detail, and use it to create our own module to provide some custom functionality to our social network.

In this chapter, you will learn:

- How to create additional content types
- More about Drupal's modular system
- How to create a module
- How to use Google Maps in our module
- More about other useful APIs available

Let's get started by discussing the module we are going to create.

Our module

We are going to create a module which leverages Google Maps to display venues which are "Dinosaur Friendly".

We are going to rapidly create the module to illustrate the power of Drupal's modular system. Modules for use in a production site should be planned in greater detail. Look up the resources, given later in this chapter, for more detail and information on how to create modules.

The module we are going to create in this chapter is designed to illustrate how modules can be created for almost any purpose to extend the functionality of a site. The module we will create provides very basic functionality. This is not a comprehensive guide to modules, that can (and does) fill entire books on its own!

Drupal's modular system

Drupal's modular system allows new functionality to be easily dropped into the web site. This keeps the functionality of the web site relevant, by allowing unnecessary features to be disabled, and new custom functionality to be slotted as the web site grows or the business needs change.

A module

A module generally makes use of the following:

- A `.info` file—this stores information about the module
- A `.module` file—this stores the functionality/business logic for the module
- A `.install` file—this tells Drupal how to install the module, including any database changes that need to be made
- Templates in our themes directory—to provide a different page layout for the module should it be required
- Additional database tables—to store the additional data related to the relevant content types

Useful resources

The following resources provide further information, in greater detail on developing modules:

- *Drupal Module Development by Matt Butcher*, published by Packt Publishing, May 2008 (`http://www.packtpub.com/drupal-6-module-development/book`)
- `http://api.drupal.org` which explains in detail the Drupal API
- The Drupal web site and the relevant developer handbooks contained within (`http://www.drupal.org/` and `http://drupal.org/node/508`)

Now that we have looked into the components involved in creating a module, and are aware of additional useful resources, we can get started with building our module!

Creating our module

We need to create our module in the following steps:

- Sign up for Google Maps for an API key
- Create the template files for the design and layout of the modules user interface
- Create the various module files to make the module work
- View our module in action

Important disclaimer

The modules created in this chapter are done very fast, to illustrate how easy it is to extend Drupal's functionality to almost any purpose. It is not an example of how a module should be created, as it does not follow many of the Drupal best practices. For full details on creating modules, you should review the resources mentioned earlier.

Content types

Most content is an extension of one of the core Drupal concepts—**the node**. To create the content types, we need to create additional database tables, which reference the node tables and contain additional information relevant to our specific content types. We also need to tell Drupal that the new types of content are available.

New content types

Venues will obviously be content types in their own right, as they will need to store information about the venue, such as name, description and coordinates. Since we are plotting these on a map, we need to create a map content type, as this will store information such as the default location of the map, and in theory would allow us to create multiple maps, for different areas. To create content types, we would log in to Drupal, as an administrator, and navigate to **Administer | Content management | Content types**. From here, we then need to click the **Add content type** link, which will take us to the form allowing us to create a new content type.

This form allows us to specify:

- A name for the content type and a machine-readable name for the content type
- A description for the content type, within the **Identification** section of the form
- A new label for the **title** field
- A new label for the **body** field (both these fields are part of the node, but we can rename them to match the context of our module)
- Minimum number of words for the body value to be valid and an explanation of the content type to be displayed at the top, all within the **Submission form settings** section of the form
- **Workflow settings** (is the content published, promoted to the front page, or sticky, or is it a new version of existing content when it is created, and are attachments enabled or disabled?)
- **Comment settings** for the content type

 While this form allows us to create new content types, the new content types will actually be created automatically when we install the modules that we are going to create!

Map

The page with our map on it will make use of a content type called map. The main reason for this is so we can easily utilize a separate template for the map page, but it also means we could expand the module to incorporate a number of maps, perhaps for specific geographical regions.

Database

Drupal takes care of common functionality of nodes, such as ensuring the title of the page appears at the top of the page, and making sure a node appears if it has been set to "published". We don't have to write this functionality from scratch. All we have to do is code the behavior that is unique to our module. This behavior depends on some custom fields, which we must make provisions for:

- The longitude and latitude coordinates to position the center of the map
- The zoom level to be used
- The dimensions of the map

These fields need to go into a new database table. Let's look at how this database table would be structured.

Field	Type	Notes
vid	Int	Content elements version ID
nid	Int	Reference to the relevant node ID in the nodes table
Longitude	Float	The longitude component of the central geographical coordinate
Latitude	Float	The latitude component of the central geographical coordinate
Zoom	Int	The level of zoom to be used in the Google Map
Width	Int	The width of the Google Map to be displayed
Height	Int	The height of the Google Map to be displayed

Later in the chapter, we will convert this structure into a format that is automatically converted into a database table when we install the module.

Venue

A venue will be used in two different ways. Firstly, the map will pull in relevant places and put them onto the map. Secondly, when a user clicks on a point on the map, he/she will be taken to a page with more information about the venue.

Database

Since all content is based on the concept of a node, we already have fields in place to give the place an ID number, a name, and a description as discussed with the map content types. However, we also need to make provisions for the longitude and latitude coordinates of the venue for its position on the map, and for the generation of the static map on the venue's own page

These fields need to go into a new database table. Let's look at how this database table would be structured:

Field	Type	Notes
vid	Int	Version ID of the content
nid	Int	Reference to the node ID in the nodes table
Longitude	Float	The longitude component of the geographical coordinates of the places
Latitude	Float	The latitude component of the geographical coordinates of the places

As with the map database, we will convert this structure into a format that is automatically converted into a database table when we install the module later in the chapter.

Google Maps

Google provide access to an API which allows developers to integrate their mapping services in innovative and interactive ways into applications and web sites. We can integrate a map to display nearby venues which are dinosaur-friendly, so our users can use the web site to look up places where they can take their dinosaurs. Other users can plot venues they have visited, but not listed, on the map for the others to see.

API key and the JavaScript files

To use the Google Maps API, we need to request an API key. This is used to control access to the API to prevent abuse. The key is restricted on a per-domain basis. So we need one key for our **http://localhost/** development site and another when the site is deployed.

To request an API key, we just need to enter our site's URL into the form on the signup page: `http://code.google.com/apis/maps/signup.html/`.

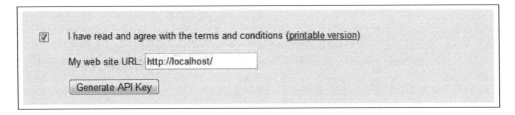

Google then presents us with an API key, a reminder of the URL it is valid for, and an example web page to use the API in. Let's make a note of the API key we were given, as we will need it later.

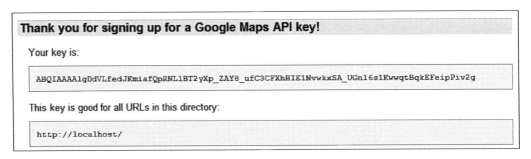

Template files

One way we can change the design of a page on a per-content type basis is by creating a template for each node type, which is loaded depending on the type of node we are viewing, and naming it `node-nodetype.tpl.php`. So, we would need the following template files:

- `node-map.tpl.php` for our map
- `node-venue.tpl.php` for our venue

These templates are stored within our themes directory: `/themes/themename/`.

node-map.tpl.php

The `node-map.tpl.php` file will be the design and layout template for the content of type "map", which will display a map of a particular region on the page with a number of places plotted on it.

```php
<?php
// $Id: node.tpl.php,v 1.5 2007/10/11 09:51:29 goba Exp $
?>
<div id="node-<?php print $node->nid; ?>"
  class="node<?php if ($sticky) { print ' sticky'; } ?>
  <?php if (!$status) { print ' node-unpublished'; } ?>">
<?php print $picture ?>

<?php if ($page == 0): ?>
  <h2><a href="<?php print $node_url ?>"
  title="<?php print $title ?>"><?php print $title ?></a></h2>
<?php endif; ?>

  <?php if ($submitted): ?>
    <span class="submitted"><?php print $submitted; ?></span>
  <?php endif; ?>

  <div class="content clear-block">
    <!-- map -->
      <div id="map" style="width: <?php print $node->width; ?>px;
        height: <?php print $node->height; ?>px"><p>content</p>
      </div>
    <?php print $content ?>
  </div>

  <div class="clear-block">
    <div class="meta">
    <?php if ($taxonomy): ?>
      <div class="terms"><?php print $terms ?></div>
```

```
<?php endif;?>
</div>

<?php if ($links): ?>
  <div class="links"><?php print $links; ?></div>
<?php endif; ?>
  </div>
</div>
```

This file is a copy of the `node.tpl.php` file, with one map related addition, which has been highlighted in the code. This change is simply a `div` (division) where the map will display.

When combined with a map in the database, and a number of places in the database, the `div` will be replaced with a Google map, which displays a specific area and plots the relevant points on the map. When a user clicks the point on the map, he/she is taken to the page of the place.

node-venue.php

The `node-place.tpl.php` file will be the design and layout template for the content of the type "venue", which will display information on a dinosaur-friendly place. This file is again a copy of the `node.tpl.php` file, with the following added above the `$content line`.

```php
<?php
// $Id: node.tpl.php,v 1.5 2007/10/11 09:51:29 goba Exp $
?>
<div id="node-<?php print $node->nid; ?>"
  class="node<?php if ($sticky) { print ' sticky'; } ?>
  <?php if (!$status) { print ' node-unpublished'; } ?>">

<?php print $picture ?>

<?php if ($page == 0): ?>
  <h2><a href="<?php print $node_url ?>"
    title="<?php print $title ?>"><?php print $title ?></a></h2>
<?php endif; ?>

  <?php if ($submitted): ?>
    <span class="submitted"><?php print $submitted; ?></span>
  <?php endif; ?>

  <div class="content clear-block">
  <!-- map -->
    <p>
  <img src="http://maps.google.com/staticmap?center=<?php print
    $node->latitude; ?>,<?php print $node->longitude; ?>
    &markers=<?php print $node->latitude; ?>,
```

```
        <?php print $node->longitude; ?>,
        red&zoom=12&size=600x150
        &key=ABQIAAAAlgDdVLfedJKmiafQpRNLlBT2yXp_ZAY8_
        ufC3CFXhHIElNvwkxSA_UGnl6s1KwwqtBqkEFeipPiv2g" alt="Map" />
    </p>
      <?php print $content ?>
    </div>
    <div class="clear-block">
      <div class="meta">
      <?php if ($taxonomy): ?>
        <div class="terms"><?php print $terms ?></div>
      <?php endif;?>
      </div>
      <?php if ($links): ?>
        <div class="links"><?php print $links; ?></div>
      <?php endif; ?>
    </div>
  </div>
```

This generates a static (not a JavaScript) map of the place on the page. Below this is then the description/comment left by the user who created the venue.

Module files

Although the map and venue functions have been referenced earlier as a single module, they will in fact be two modules. So a more accurate definition would be that they are a module package. Both modules will be required; we just need to physically separate things into two separate modules in order to get things working as required.

Directories and locations

Each of our two modules requires a directory to contain the relevant files related to them. For the moment, we will create the relevant folders outside our Drupal environment, while we develop the modules. We need to create a folder called map and a folder called venue. Once finished, we will put the files into our Drupal installation.

.info files

As discussed earlier, the .info files contain information about the module, including its name, its compatibility with PHP and Drupal, and a description of the module. We can also provide a value for the modules package. This groups the modules together in the administration panel.

Map module (map.info)

The map.info file describes the map module in a few lines.

```
; $Id$
name = "Map Overview"
description = "Display a map of dinosaur friendly venues"
core = 6.x
php = 5.1
package = DinoMaps
```

The php and package lines are optional, though the package line ensures that the map and venue modules are grouped together.

Venue module (venue.info)

The venue.info file describes the venue module in a few lines. Note that the two info files have the same package value to ensure that they are grouped together.

```
; $Id$
name = "Venue Detail"
description = "Display information on a specific dinosaur friendly
Venue"
core = 6.x
php = 5.1
package = DinoMaps
```

.module files

The relevant .module files for our modules store the core functionality of the modules and define how they work and behave. Our .module files need to:

- Implement hook_helphook_help for the admin area to display a help line of text
- Display the relevant fields in the insert/update forms for the extra database data
- Insert data into the relevant database tables when a new content element of this type is created

- Update date in the relevant tables when a content element of this type is edited
- Delete relevant database records when a content element of this type is deleted
- Implement `hook_nodeapi` to allow individual revisions to be deleted
- Implement `hook_load` to load the custom node data
- Implement `hook_view` so that the frontend can access the node data
- Define permissions for the modules
- Control access based on these permissions

These "hooks" allow modules to interact with the Drupal core. More information is available at `http://api.drupal.org/api/group/hooks`.

Map module (map.module)

We need the map module to do the following:

- Generate a map
- Generate a list of places
- Plot the places on the map
- Provide a link to details on places

The module code for this, `map.module`, is shown below. Let's review it before we look at how it works.

```
<?php
// $Id$
/**
 * @file
 * Module for map
 */
 /**
 * Implementation of hook_help().
 */
 function map_help($path, $arg) {
    if( $path == 'admin/help#map' )    b{
      $txt = 'This module displays the map of venues page. It assumes
             the existence of a content type named map';
   }

   return '<p>' . $txt . '</p>';
 }
```

```
function map_node_info() {
  return array(
    'map' => array(
    'name' => t('Map Details'),
    'module' => 'map',
    'description' => t('A map of venues page.'),
    'has_title' => TRUE,
    'title_label' => t('Map Name'),
    'has_body' => TRUE,
    'body_label' => t('Map body'),
    )
  );
}

function map_form(&$node)    {
  $type = node_get_types( 'type', $node );
  if($type->has_title)    {
    $form['title'] = array(
      '#type' => 'textfield',
      '#title' => check_plain( $type->title_label),
      '#required' =>TRUE,
      '#default_value' => $node->title,
      '#weight' => -5,
    );
  }
  if($type->has_body) {
    $form['body_field'] = node_body_field(
      $node,
      $type->body_label,
      $type->min_word_count
    );
  }

  $form['longitude'] = array(
    '#type' => 'textfield',
    '#title' => t('Central point longitude'),
    '#required' =>TRUE,
    '#default_value' => 0,
  );
  $form['latitude'] = array(
    '#type' => 'textfield',
    '#title' => t('Central point latitude'),
    '#required' =>TRUE,
    '#default_value' => 0,
```

```
    );
    $form['zoom'] = array(
        '#type' => 'textfield',
        '#title' => t('Zoom Level'),
        '#required' =>TRUE,
        '#default_value' => 0,
    );
    $form['width'] = array(
        '#type' => 'textfield',
        '#title' => t('Map Width'),
        '#required' =>TRUE,
        '#default_value' => 0,
    );
    $form['height'] = array(
        '#type' => 'textfield',
        '#title' => t('Map Height'),
        '#required' =>TRUE,
        '#default_value' => 0,
    );
    return $form;
}

/**
 * Insert hook for when new maps are added.
 */
function map_insert($node) {

    // Insert the custom data in $node into the map table.

$sql = sprintf(
    'INSERT INTO {maps} (nid, longitude, latitude, zoom, width,
        height) ' .
    "VALUES (%d, '%s', '%s', '%s', '%s', '%s' )",
    $node->nid,
    $node->longitude,
    $node->latitude,
    $node->zoom,
    $node->width,
    $node->height);

    db_query($sql);
  // maybe: menu_link_save?
}
```

```
/**
 * Implementation of hook_update, for when a map node is updated.
 */
function map_update($node)    {
  if ($node->revision)
  {
   map_insert($node);
  }
  else
  {
    db_query(
      "UPDATE {maps}" .
      "SET longitude = '%s', latitude = '%s', zoom = '%s',
          width = '%s', height = '%s' " .
      "WHERE nid = %d",
      $node->longitude,
      $node->latitude,
      $node->zoom,
      $node->width,
      $node->height,
      $node->nid
    );
  }
}
/**
 * Implementation of hook_delete, for when a map node is deleted.
 */
function map_delete($node) {
  db_query(
    "DELETE FROM {maps} WHERE nid = %d",
    $node->nid
  );
}
/**
 * Implementation of hook_nodeapi, for when individual revisions
    need to be deleted.
 */
function map_nodeapi(&$node, $op, $teaser, $page) {
  if ($op == "delete revision")
  {
    db_query(
      "DELETE FROM (maps) WHERE nid = %d",
      $node->nid
    );
```

```
      }
    }


/**
 * Implementation of hook_load for our custom data.
 */
function map_load($node) {

      $sql = sprintf(
        "SELECT longitude, latitude, zoom, width, height " .
    "FROM {maps} WHERE nid = %d",
    $node->nid);
      $result = db_query($sql);
  $obj = db_fetch_object($result);

  return $obj;

}
/**
 * Implementation of hook_view for our custom data
 */
function map_view($node, $teaser = FALSE, $page = FALSE) {
  $node = node_prepare($node, $teaser);
  drupal_set_html_head("<script src=\"http://maps.google.com/maps?
    file=api&amp;v=2&amp;
    key=ABQIAAAAlgDdVLfedJKmiafQpRNLlBT2yXp
      _ZAY8_ufC3CFXhHIE1NvwkxSA_UGnl6s1KwwqtBqkEFeipPiv2g\"
    type=\"text/javascript\"></script>");
  $mapjs = "<script type=\"text/javascript\">
              //<![CDATA[

  function load() {
    if (GBrowserIsCompatible()) {
      var map = new GMap2(document.getElementById(\"map\"));
      map.setCenter(new GLatLng(".$node->latitude.",
                          ".$node->longitude."),
                          ".$node->zoom.");

      function createMarker(latlng, nid) {
        var marker = new GMarker(latlng);
        marker.value = nid;
       GEvent.addListener(marker,\"click\", function() {
        window.location = 'http://localhost/drupal-6.9/node/' + nid
        });
        return marker;
}";
```

```
$node->venues = array();
$result = db_query("SELECT nid, longitude,
 latitude FROM {venues}");
while ($venue = db_fetch_object($result))
{
   $node->venue[] = array( 'nid' => $venue->nid,
                           'longitude' => $venue->longitude,
                           'latitude' => $venue->latitude );
   $mapjs .= "var latlng = new GLatLng(" . $venue->latitude .",
                                 ".$venue->longitude.");
 map.addOverlay(createMarker(latlng, ".$venue->nid."));";
}
$mapjs .= " }
}
//]]>
window.onload = function () {
load();
}
window.unload = function () {
GUnload();
}
</script>";

drupal_set_html_head( $mapjs );

return $node;
}
function map_perm() {
   return array(
      'create map node',
      'edit map nodes',
      'delete map nodes',
   );
}
function map_access($op, $node, $account) {
   switch( $op )
   {
      case 'create':
      return user_access('create map node', $account );
      case 'update':
      return user_access('edit map nodes', $account );
      case 'delete':
      return user_access('delete map nodes', $account );
   }
}
```

Venue module

We need the venue module to:

- Display information about a venue
- Display a small, static map of the location

Let's look at how this would be done:

```php
<?php
// $Id$
/**
 * @file
 * Module for venue
 */
 /**
 * Implementation of hook_help()
 */
function venue_help($path, $arg) {
  if( $path == 'admin/help#venue' )
  {
    $txt = 'This module displays the details of venue page. It
      assumes the existence of a content type named venue';
  }
  return '<p>' . $txt . '</p>';
}

function venue_node_info()  {
  return array(
    'venue' => array(
      'name' => t('venue Details'),
    'module' => 'venue',
    'description' => t('A venue page.'),
     'has_title' => TRUE,
      'title_label' => t('venue Name'),
    'has_body' => TRUE,
    'body_label' => t('venue body'),
     )
  );
}

function venue_form(&$node)  {

  $type = node_get_types( 'type', $node );
  if($type->has_title)    {
    $form['title'] = array(
```

```
          '#type' => 'textfield',
          '#title' => check_plain( $type->title_label),
          '#required' =>TRUE,
          '#default_value' => $node->title,
          '#weight' => -5,
      );
  }
  if( $type->has_body ) {
    $form['body_field'] = node_body_field(
      $node,
      $type->body_label,
      $type->min_word_count
    );
  }

  $form['longitude'] = array(
     '#type' => 'textfield',
       '#title' => t('Venue longitude'),
     '#required' =>TRUE,
     '#default_value' => 0,
  );

  $form['latitude'] = array(
     '#type' => 'textfield',
       '#title' => t('Venue latitude'),
     '#required' =>TRUE,
     '#default_value' => 0,
  );

  return $form;
}

/**
 * Insert hook for when new venues are added.
 */
function venue_insert($node) {
  // Insert the custom data in $node into the venues table.
  $sql = sprintf(
     'INSERT INTO {venues} (nid, longitude, latitude) ' .
     "VALUES (%d, '%s', '%s' )",
     $node->nid,
     $node->longitude,
     $node->latitude);
```

```
    db_query($sql);
  // maybe: menu_link_save?
}
/**
 * Implementation of hook_update, for when a venue node is updated.
 */
function venue_update($node) {
  if ($node->revision) {
   venue_insert($node);
  }
  else {
    db_query(
      "UPDATE {venues} " .
      "SET longitude = '%s', latitude = '%s' " .
      "WHERE nid = %d AND vid= %d",
     $node->longitude,
     $node->latitude,
     $node->nid,
     $node->vid
    );
  }
}
/**
 * Implementation of hook_delete, for when a venue node is deleted.
 */
function venue_delete($node) {
  db_query(
    "DELETE FROM {venues} WHERE nid = %d",
    $node->nid
  );
}
/**
 * Implementation of hook_nodeapi, for when individual revisions
   need to be deleted.
 */
function venue_nodeapi(&$node, $op, $teaser, $page) {
  if ($op == "delete revision") {
    db_query(
      "DELETE FROM (venues) WHERE nid = %d",
      $node->nid
    );
  }
}
```

```
/**
 * Implementation of hook_load for our custom data.
 */
function venue_load($node) {

    $sql = sprintf(
        "SELECT longitude, latitude " .
    "FROM {venues} WHERE nid = %d",
    $node->nid);
        $result = db_query($sql);
    $obj = db_fetch_object($result);

    return $obj;


}
/**
 * Implementation of hook_view for our custom data
 */
function venue_view($node, $teaser = FALSE, $page = FALSE)    {
    $node = node_prepare($node, $teaser);
    return $node;
}
function venue_perm()
{
    return array(
        'create venue node',
        'edit venue nodes',
        'delete venue nodes',
    );
}
function venue_access($op, $node, $account)
{
    switch( $op )
    {
        case 'create':
            return user_access('create venue node', $account );
            case 'update':
            return user_access('edit venue nodes', $account );
            case 'delete':
            return user_access('delete venue nodes', $account );
    }
}
```

.install files

For the .install files, we need to convert our database structures for the relevant modules, into schemas compatible with the Drupal schema API. The .install file is used when a module is installed or uninstalled via the **administration** area, and can be used to easily add new tables to the Drupal database.

The .install files contain three main sections:

- An implementation of hook_install
- An implementation of hook_schema
- An implementation of hook_uninstall

The hook_schema implementation returns an array consisting of the database structure. The install and uninstall implementations apply and undo the changes defined in the schema implementation, making it easy to install and remove modules at the click of a button via the administration area. More information on the schema API is available on http://api.drupal.org/api/group/schemaapi/6 and http://drupal.org/node/146939, as well as in the *Drupal Module Development book*, http://www.packtpub.com/drupal-6-module-development/book.

Map module (map.install)

This is essentially the database structure we discussed earlier for the map module in the Drupal database schema.

```php
<?php
// $Id$
/**
 * Implementation of hook_install().
 */
function map_install() {
  drupal_install_schema('map');
}
/**
 * Implementation of hook_uninstall().
 */
function map_uninstall() {
  drupal_uninstall_schema('map');
}
/**
 * Implementation of hook_schema().
 */
function map_schema() {
```

```php
$schema['maps'] = array(
  'fields' => array(
    'vid' => array(
      'type' => 'int',
      'unsigned' => TRUE,
      'not null' => TRUE,
      'default' => 0
    ),
    'nid' => array(
      'type' => 'int',
      'unsigned' => TRUE,
      'not null' => TRUE,
      'default' => 0
    ),
    'longitude' => array(
      'type' => 'float',
      'not null' => TRUE,
      'default' => 0
    ),
    'latitude' => array(
      'type' => 'float',
      'not null' => TRUE,
      'default' => 0
    ),
    'zoom' => array(
      'type' => 'int',
      'unsigned' => TRUE,
      'not null' => TRUE,
      'default' => 0
    ),
    'width' => array(
      'type' => 'int',
      'unsigned' => TRUE,
      'not null' => TRUE,
      'default' => 0
    ),
    'height' => array(
      'type' => 'int',
      'unsigned' => TRUE,
      'not null' => TRUE,
      'default' => 0
    ),

  ),
```

```
      'indexes' => array(
        'nid' => array('nid'),
      ),
      'primary key' => array('vid'),
    );
    return $schema;
}
```

Venue module (venue.install)

This is essentially the database structure we discussed earlier for the place module in the Drupal database schema.

```
<?php
// $Id$
/**
 * Implementation of hook_install().
 */
function venue_install() {
  drupal_install_schema('venue');
}
/**
 * Implementation of hook_uninstall().
 */
function venue_uninstall() {
  drupal_uninstall_schema('venue');
}
/**
 * Implementation of hook_schema().
 */
function venue_schema() {
  $schema['venues'] = array(
    'fields' => array(
      'vid' => array(
        'type' => 'int',
        'unsigned' => TRUE,
        'not null' => TRUE,
        'default' => 0
      ),
      'nid' => array(
        'type' => 'int',
        'unsigned' => TRUE,
        'not null' => TRUE,
        'default' => 0
```

```
        ),
        'longitude' => array(
          'type' => 'float',
          'not null' => TRUE,
          'default' => 0
        ),
        'latitude' => array(
          'type' => 'float',
          'not null' => TRUE,
          'default' => 0
        ),
      ),
      'indexes' => array(
        'nid' => array('nid'),
      ),
      'primary key' => array('vid'),
    );

    return $schema;
}
```

Putting everything together

We have now created our basic module, let's look at how it all fits together, and start using the module!

Installing the modules

We have installed a lot of modules over the previous chapters. So hopefully, this doesn't need to be reiterated. However, for completeness sake, here is how to install our modules:

- Move the map and venue module folders to the /sites/all/modules folder
- Move the templates into the relevant themes folder
- Enable the modules
- Use the modules

To enable the modules, we simply check the relevant boxes in the **administration** area.

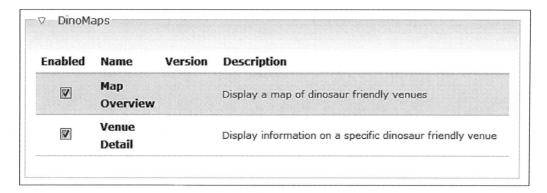

Now that our modules are enabled, we can start using the modules.

Creating a map

To create the map, we simply go to **Create content | Map**. Here, we can enter the **longitude, latitude, zoom level, width,** and **height** of the map. We would want the permissions of this to allow only administrators or active contributors to create new maps.

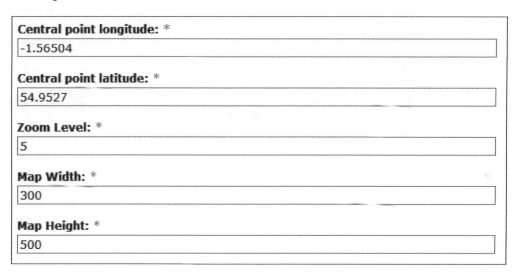

With a map created, we now need to create some places for our map!

Adding a venue

To create the venue, we simply go to **Create content | Venue** and enter the name, description and coordinates of the venue.

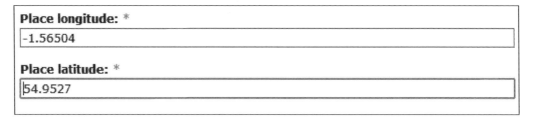

Place longitude: *
-1.56504

Place latitude: *
54.9527

Seeing the module in action

Now that we have created some content which our modules can use, we can see our module in action!

On the map, we have the place which we had added earlier. Clicking the point takes us to the place detail page, which provides further information on the place, and why it is dinosaur-friendly.

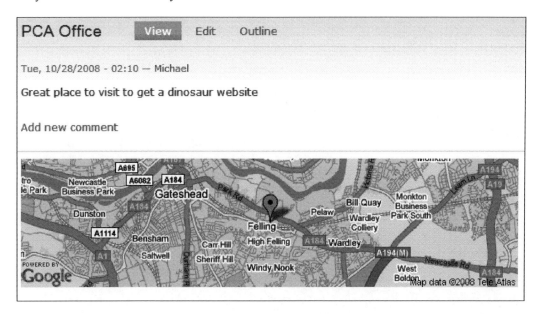

We can also set the permissions for the venues to allow users to create content of the type place, so they can share their experiences of dinosaur-friendly hotels, restaurants, cinemas, and so on.

Useful APIs

There are a number of modules for Drupal that provide a framework and APIs to other web services and applications. The following are some useful examples.

GMap

This module provides an API / framework for working with Google Maps data (although we didn't use it in this chapter).

```
http://drupal.org/project/gmap
```

Facebook

This module/API provides a wrapper that can be used by other modules, and new custom modules. There is a Facebook App module which makes use of it. So this can be used to provide core Facebook-related code.

```
http://drupal.org/project/facebook_api
```

Summary

In this chapter, we quickly explored Drupal's modular system, and used it to create two modules which added some additional functionality that is relevant and is of use to our social network. This included creating .info, .module, and .install files for the modules as well as creating additional templates and database tables for them to utilize.

8
Designing our Site

Our social networking site is feature complete, but at the moment, it resembles any other default Drupal installation, as we have kept the default theme in use. Let's take a look at how Drupal works with regards to themes and designs, and change the design of our site to something more appropriate.

In this chapter, you will learn:

- About Drupal themes
- How to customize the default theme
- The basics of creating a theme

So let's get started!

Drupal themes

The design (or "look and feel") of our site is controlled by the theme. Drupal provides us with a number of themes out of the box. Initially, one theme, which is the default, is enabled. So all users of our site experience the same look and feel. If we wish so, we can enable more than one theme, so that our users may choose the look and feel of the web site.

Themes are administered via **Administer | Site building | Themes**.

Themes and our users

The themes administration page lists all the themes available to us in our Drupal installation. To enable more than one theme for our users, we simply need to check the **Enabled** box next to the themes we wish to enable, and select the **Default** button if we wish this theme to be the default look and feel for the site.

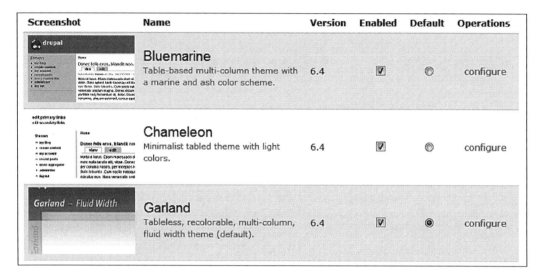

Screenshot	Name	Version	Enabled	Default	Operations
	Bluemarine Table-based multi-column theme with a marine and ash color scheme.	6.4	☑	◎	configure
	Chameleon Minimalist tabled theme with light colors.	6.4	☑	◎	configure
	Garland Tableless, recolorable, multi-column, fluid width theme (default).	6.4	☑	◉	configure

If they have permissions to do so, users can change the theme they use by editing their accounts. Grouped under **Theme configuration** is a list of the installed themes allowing the user to select the one they wish to use.

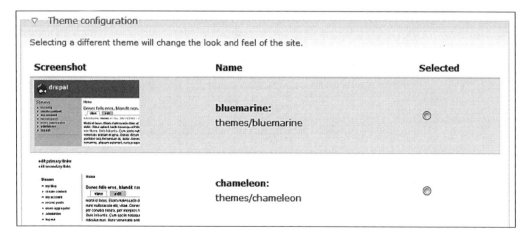

▽ Theme configuration

Selecting a different theme will change the look and feel of the site.

Screenshot	Name	Selected
	bluemarine: themes/bluemarine	◎
	chameleon: themes/chameleon	◎

The list of themes displays a thumbnail of the theme, so that the user can see at a glance and select the layout of the theme.

Pre-installed themes

By default, Drupal has the following themes installed (although all but one is disabled):

- Bluemarine
- Chameleon
- Garland
- Marvin
- Minnelli
- Pushbutton

Many of these themes are old and out-of-date, particularly with regards to the way they have been created. But there may be one which is a good starting point for a theme we wish to create. Let's have a brief look at these themes.

Bluemarine

Quite a corporate theme, this is a block-based theme with a very rigid menu and header. The layout is fluid, so the design adapts to the width of the user's web browser.

Although a corporate theme, it has a less corporate feel than the Marvin theme, and is naturally less vibrant than themes such as Minnelli and Garland.

Chameleon

This is a very simplistic theme, making use of the whitespace and a white background. Older computers with poor color schemes may be better suited to use this theme, due to the lack of colors or dependence on images to achieve the design. Mobile devices too may work well with this theme.

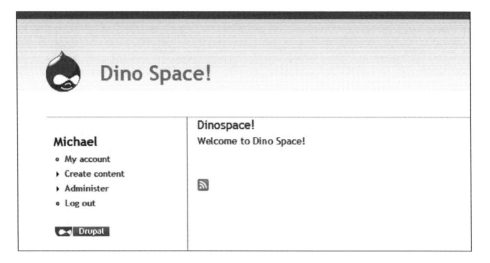

Garland

This is the theme which is set to default on new Drupal installations.

This is a fluid width theme (unlike Minnelli, which is a fixed-width version of this theme).

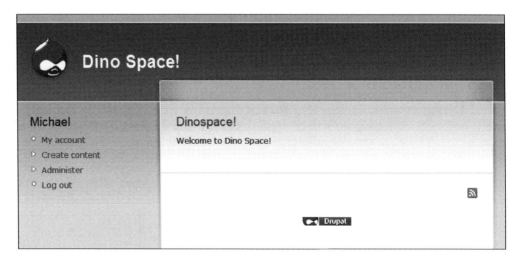

The use of gradient color schemes in the header and menu, a fresh color scheme and the glassy effect logo is a style commonly used in web site design at the moment. Overall, it gives a modern, friendly, and welcoming feel to the site.

Marvin

A very corporate and simplistic design, it is useful as a starting point for a business web site.

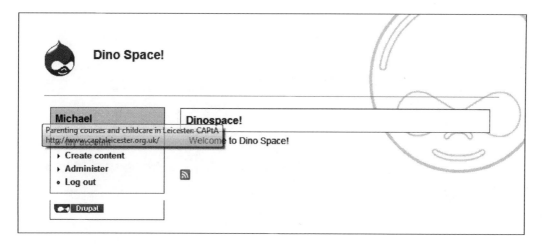

Further customization would make this theme look much better.

Minnelli

This is identical to the Garland theme, but with a fixed-width.

Pushbutton

This theme maintains a clean, professional look, and its use of typography seems to be designed with the visually impaired in mind.

Contributed themes

There are vast numbers of themes created by Drupal enthusiasts available on the Drupal web site, `http://drupal.org/project/Themes`. This web site lists available themes, as well as the Drupal version they were designed for. Screenshots of most of the themes are available, so we can see what the theme would look like.

Don't forget
When downloading themes from the Drupal web site, or elsewhere, ensure that they are compatible with the version of Drupal you have installed.

Installing contributed themes

To install a contributed theme (that is, a theme from the Drupal web site), we simply need to extract the contents of the downloaded file into the `/sites/default/themes` folder, so we can enable, and configure them from the **administration** area. The Zen theme is an excellent starting point for creating a different look from the typical Garland look.

Customizing the default theme

Most themes can be customized slightly direct from the administration area. We can customize the following features of a theme:

- The color scheme
- Which elements are used in the theme (for instance. search box)
- The logo
- The favicon or the "shortcut" icon

These settings can also be set globally for all installed themes, or individually on a per theme basis.

Themes are customized by navigating to **Administer | Site building | Themes** and then clicking the **configure** link next to the relevant theme. Let's configure the default theme!

Color scheme

The colors used by the (Garland) theme can be changed in the color scheme group of settings. There are two options for changing the colors. We can either select a preset **Color set** from the **Color set** drop-down list, or we can create a custom color set based on the colors we define.

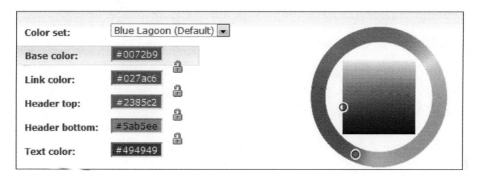

The color sets available include:

- **Blue Lagoon**—Selected by default; a bright, vibrant blue color scheme
- **Ash**—Dark grey color scheme
- **Aquamarine**—Green/Blue color scheme
- **Belgian Chocolate**—Dark red color scheme
- **Bluemarine**—Light blue color scheme; not as vibrant as blue lagoon and without a gradient
- **Citrus Blast**—Yellow color scheme
- **Cold Day**—Dark blue color scheme
- **Greenbeam**—Vibrant green color scheme
- **Mediterrano**—Orange/Red color scheme
- **Mercury**—Light grey color scheme with subtle gradient
- **Nocturnal**—Dark blue/grey color scheme
- **Olivia**—Light green color scheme with gradient
- **Pink Plastic**—Bright pink color scheme
- **Shiny Tomato**—Red color scheme
- **Teal Top**—Teal color scheme
- **Custom**—Allows us to select colors of our own choice

Personally I like the **Mercury** color scheme, so I will use that for Dino Space.

Custom color sets

We can also define our own color set by selecting custom from the list. With the custom set selected, we should click in the relevant color box we wish to change, and click the color on the color wheel, which will then update the color used by the set.

Color set preview

The preview section beneath the settings for the color scheme updates to reflect the colors we have set, for instance, if we select **Mercury** as the color scheme, the **Preview** image updates to the following:

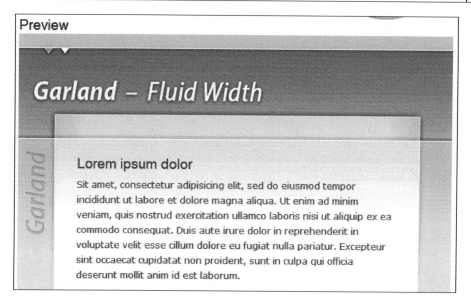

Toggle display

The next group of settings is **Toggle display**, which allows us to select which additional elements of the theme are enabled. For instance, if we have the search module installed, we can select if a **Search box** is shown within the theme or not.

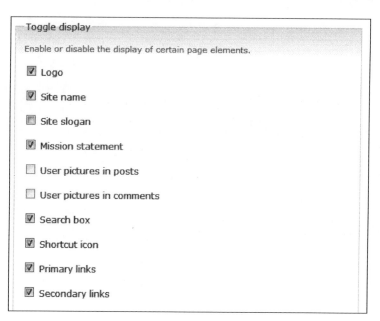

Boxes which are disabled (that is, where we cannot check them) are related to features which are not enabled (for instance, if the search module was not enabled, we could not enable the display of the **Search box**).

Logo image design

At the top of the page, we have the Drupal logo. We can easily change this to a logo of our own choice, by uploading it from this area.

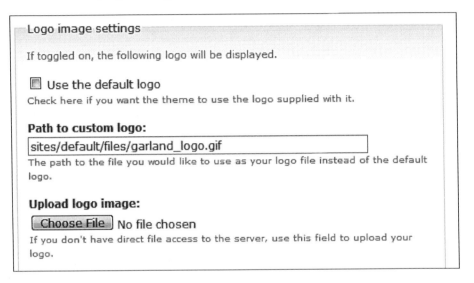

Once a logo has been uploaded, it is then reflected in the web site, as demonstrated with my poorly designed logo below:

Shortcut icon settings

When you visit a web site, there is often a small version of the logo displayed next to the web address in the address bar; this is called a favicon. Similarly for uploading the icon, we can upload a favicon from the admin area.

The first stage in setting this icon is to actually create the icon file. Thankfully, there are a number of free online tools such as `http://tools.dynamicdrive.com/favicon/` which allow us to upload an image and convert it into a favicon, which we can then upload to our site.

Global settings

A number of the settings we have looked into with our default theme can be configured on a global basis for all the available themes.

The settings which can be configured globally include:

- Toggle display (including a few extra ones not available in the default skin, as not all elements are supported by all skins)
- Content which contains additional post information
- Logo image settings
- Shortcut icon settings

Creating a theme: The basics

Creating a theme is a very large topic, and here we are going to cover it only very briefly. For more detailed information, please consider the following:

- Drupal Theme Guide - `http://drupal.org/theme-guide`
- *Drupal 6 Themes* by Ric Shreves, published by Packt Publishing (`http://www.packtpub.com/drupal-6-themes/book`)

 Knowledge of HTML, CSS and some PHP would be very beneficial for this section.

Important disclaimer

The theme we create here is designed to illustrate how to create a theme quickly, based on an existing template. It is not designed to be a guide on best practices for theme design and creation. The resources mentioned earlier should help as a more comprehensive guide to creating themes. This just illustrates how easy it is to change the design of a Drupal site. When making this theme, you may wish to set your administrative theme to Garland, so that any changes made by the theme don't affect the administration area, so you can easily disable the theme if need be.

Theme structure

A theme is made up of the following files:

- An info file, which is required
- Template files
- A template.php (optional)
- A logo and a screenshot (optional)

Info file

This is a configuration file, which is named with the same name as the theme, with the extension .info, for example, dinospacetheme.info. An example .info file is shown below:

```
name = Dinospacetheme
description = Theme for the dinospace website
version = 1
core = 6.x
engine = phptemplate
stylesheets[all][] = style.css
```

This tells Drupal that our theme is called Dinospacetheme, that it is compatible with Drupal 6, and that the main style sheet which it will use is called style.css.

Template files

The main aspect of a theme is of course, the templates files themselves. These contain the HTML which makes up the sites design, as well as PHP code to dynamically insert content, menus, and other site information. We need to create the following template files:

- `page.tpl.php`
- `node.tpl.php`
- `comment.tpl.php`
- `block.tpl.php`

The `page.tpl.php` file is for pages, the `node.tpl.php` is for all nodes and content, and is inserted dynamically into the `page.tpl.php` template; the `comment.tpl.php` is for comments and `block.tpl.php` is for any blocks that may be displayed.

Template.php

The `template.php` isn't required, and can be used to store any conditional logic, or pre-process functions (`http://drupal.org/node/223430`). We are not going to use a `template.php` file in our theme.

Logo and screenshot

A screenshot helps users get a quick preview of the theme, if they are considering using it, and can also help remind us (administrators) as to what the theme is, if we were to change the themes that are enabled, at a later date. The logo is the logo shown in the header.

Other files for themes

Themes can consist of more than what we have already mentioned. For instance, we could create sub-themes, in which case, a theme would need to contain the sub themes. Themes can also contain color variations, in which case, we would need a `color` directory containing a `color.inc` file.

Getting started

One of the easiest ways to get started is to copy the default theme and replace the files within it with the files for the new theme by taking an HTML template for a design, and breaking this apart to form the various template files we need. We are going to use the template as shown in the following screenshot:

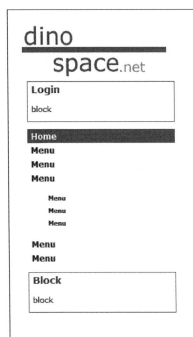

This template has the following HTML:

```
<!DOCTYPE html PUBLIC "-//W3C//DTD XHTML 1.0 Strict//EN"
  "http://www.w3.org/TR/xhtml1/DTD/xhtml1-strict.dtd">
<html xmlns="http://www.w3.org/1999/xhtml" xml:lang="en" lang="en">
<head>
  <title>pagetitle</title>
  <meta http-equiv="content-type" content="text/html;
      charset=iso-8859-1" />

  <style type="text/css" title="Default page style" media="screen">
  <!--@import "ds.css";--></style>
  <style type="text/css" media="screen">
  #nav li.home a {background: #2266BB !important;color:
    #FFF !important}
  </style>
```

```
    <link rel="icon" href="favicon.ico" type="image/x-icon" />
    <link rel="shortcut icon" href="favicon.ico" type="image/x-icon" />
</head>
<body id="">
<div id="wrapper">
<div id="main">
<div id="column">
<a href="#" title="">
<img src="images/dslogo.gif" alt="" />
</a>
<div id="nav">
<div class="block">
<h2>Login</h2>
<p>block</p>
</div>
<ul>
<li class="home"><a rel="nofollow" href="#" title="">Home</a></li>
<li><a rel="nofollow" href="" title="">Menu</a></li>
<li><a rel="nofollow" href="" title="">Menu</a></li>
<li><a rel="nofollow" href="" title="">Menu</a></li>
<ul>
<li><a rel="nofollow" href="" title="">Menu</a></li>
<li><a rel="nofollow" href="" title="">Menu</a></li>
<li><a rel="nofollow" href="" title="">Menu</a></li>
</ul>
</li>
<li><a rel="nofollow" href="" title="">Menu</a></li>
<li><a rel="nofollow" href="" title="">Menu</a></li>
</ul>
<div class="block">
<h2>Block</h2>
<p>block</p>
</div>
</div><!--/nav-->
</div><!--/column-->
<div id="main-content">
<div id="header">
</div><!--/header-->
<div id="content">
<h1>Welcome to Dino Space!</h1>
<p>
Donec ut leo. Aenean justo. Nam risus ante, malesuada ut, blandit id.
</p>
<p>
```

```
Nulla quam sem, consequat vel, dapibus sit amet, tristique nec, justo.
Nulla facilisi. Fusce risus sem, blandit eu, consectetuer sed, gravida
a, dolor. Sed ut felis vitae urna tempus imperdiet.
</p>
<h2>What is Dino Space?</h2>
<p>
Duis venenatis. Etiam eget elit. Nulla fermentum tincidunt arcu. In
tincidunt lectus in dui. Donec semper venenatis orci. Cras iaculis
porta velit. Nam congue. Ut pulvinar condimentum magna. Vestibulum in
dui in libero condimentum mollis.
</p>
<p>
Suspendisse tortor. Duis nec nisl. Nam rutrum tincidunt ligula.
Vivamus congue feugiat nisi. Vestibulum vehicula viverra est.
Suspendisse non enim non diam tempor vulputate. Ut enim eros, sodales
vel, facilisis ut, mattis non, ante.
</p>
</div><!--/content-->
<div id="footer">
<p>
<a href="http://www.peacockcarter.co.uk/web-design" title="Web
designers Newcastle">Web design Newcastle</a> by <a href="http://www.
peacockcarter.co.uk/" title="Peacock Carter, North East web designers
in Newcastle">Peacock Carter</a>
</p>
</div><!--/footer-->
</div><!--/main-content-->
<div class="clear"></div>
</div><!--/main-->
</div><!--/wrapper-->
</body>
</html>
```

The following CSS is used in the template:

```
/* peacockcarter.co.uk 2006 - 2009 [ds] */
/* Reset */
address, caption, cite, code, dfn, th{font-style:normal; font-weight:
normal}
abbr, acronym{border:0}
body, html{margin: 0; padding: 0;}
blockquote, body, div, dl, dt, dd, fieldset, form, h1, h2, h3, h4, h5,
h6, input, li, ol, ul, p, pre, textarea, td, th{margin:0; padding:0}
caption, th{text-align:left}
h1, h2, h3, h4, h5, h6, p, pre, blockquote{background:transparent;
font-weight:normal; word-spacing:0px}
```

```
fieldset, img{border:0}
table{border-collapse:collapse; border-spacing:0; clear:both;
margin:10px; width: 525px !important}
/* Generic */
a, a:active, a:link,a:visited{background:transparent; color: #000;
font-weight: bold;text-decoration:underline}
a:hover{color:#2266BB; text-decoration: none}
abbr, acronym, dfn{border-bottom-width:1px; border-bottom-style:
dotted; cursor:help}
address{color:#000; font-size:0.7em; line-height:1.8em}
blockquote {}
body{background: #FFF;color:#000; font-family: arial, verdana,
helvetica,sans-serif; font-size: 62.5%;}
caption{font-size:0.8em; font-weight:bold}
em{font-style:italic}
.float_left{float:left !important}
.float_none{float:none !important}
.float_right{float:right !important}
.clear{clear: both !important}
.hide {display: none !important}
#nav,h1,h2,h3,h4,h5,h6 {font-family: verdana, sans-serif}
h1 a, h2 a, h3 a, h4 a, h5 a, h6 a, h1 acronym, h1 abbr{border-bottom-
width:0px !important; text-decoration: none !important}
h1 a:hover, h2 a:hover, h3 a:hover, h4 a:hover, h5 a:hover, h6 a:
hover{text-decoration: underline !important}
h1{color: #2266BB;font-size:250%;letter-spacing:0; line-
height:110%;margin: 0;padding: 0}
h2 {color:#555; font-size: 200%;font-weight:bold; letter-spacing:0;
line-height:150%}
h3{color:#666; font-size:175%; font-weight:bold; letter-
spacing:1px;line-height:100%;margin-top: 5px}
h4, h5, h6{color:#555; font-size:1.1em; font-weight:bold; letter-
spacing:1px;line-height:1.5em;margin-top: 5px}
h2 a, h3 a {color: #555 !important; font-weight: inherit !important;}
p, address {text-align:justify}
ul{list-style-type:square}
strong{font-weight:bold}
caption{display: none}
th, td {padding: 5px}
th {background: #2266BB;color: #FFF;font-weight: bold}
td {color: #555}
/* Layout */
#wrapper {
background: #FFF;
margin: 25px auto 0 auto;
```

```css
padding: 0 0 75px 0;
width: 800px
}
#logo {}
#header {color: #000;height: 80px}

#nav {
float: left;
font-size: 100%;
height: 52px;
}
  #nav ul {
  list-style-type: none;
  }
  #nav li a {
  color: #330033;
  display: block;
  font-weight: bold;
  padding: 2px 5px;
  text-decoration: none;
  width: 210px;
  }
  #nav li a:hover {
    color: #2266BB;
    }
  ul ul {
  font-size: 75%;
  margin-left: 0 !important;
  padding-left: 25px !important;
  }
  ul ul li {border-bottom: 2px #FFF dotted;}
  ul ul li a {margin-left: 0 !important;width: 175px !important}

.block { margin-left: 25px; padding-left: 5px; border: 1px solid
#2266BB; }
.block h2 {color:#555; font-size: 120%;font-weight:bold; letter-
spacing:0; line-height:150%}
/* Main */
#main {clear: both;font-size: 120%}
  #main p, #main ul, #main dl, #main ol {
  font-weight: normal;
  line-height: 135%;
  margin: 10px 0;
  }
```

```
    #main-content img {float: right;margin: 5px 0 5px 10px}
    #main ul, #main dl, #main ol {margin-left: 25px}
#main-content {
float: left;
width: 475px
}
    #content {background: #FFF;padding: 10px 25px}
#column {
background: transparent;
float: left;
padding: 10px;
width: 250px;
}
    #column p {font-size: 90%;text-align: left}
    #column img {float: right}
#footer {
background: #FFF;
clear: both;
color: #CCC;
font-size: 90%;
height: 105px;
padding: 5px 10px 0 10px
}
    #footer p {padding: 0 100px 0 25px}
    #footer a {color: #CCC}
    #footer a:hover {color: #CCC}
```

We will need to break the HTML up into a number of template files, and insert the relevant PHP code to ensure that Drupal adds in our sites content. As this template was not designed with Drupal in mind, we may need to make changes to bits of it, as we go along.

Info file

We are going to create a theme called dstheme, which will use the phptemplate engine. So our .info file will be called dstheme.info and will contain the following:

```
name = dstheme
description = Theme for the dinospace website
version = 1
core = 6.x
engine = phptemplate
stylesheets[all][] = ds.css
```

Template files

One way to build the template files from the template HTML from earlier is to take the HTML and save it as page.tpl.php and place into it, some of the PHP code from the page.tpl.php file in the Garland theme. If we do this, and then install the theme, we should see how well Drupal links in with our HTML template, and also what we need to change to accommodate Drupal better.

Page.tpl.php

By merging the PHP from the Garland page.tpl.php file into our HTML template from earlier, we get this as the page.tpl.php file for our new theme. The PHP code which has been inserted is highlighted.

```
<!DOCTYPE html PUBLIC "-//W3C//DTD XHTML 1.0 Strict//EN"
   "http://www.w3.org/TR/xhtml1/DTD/xhtml1-strict.dtd">
<html xmlns="http://www.w3.org/1999/xhtml" xml:lang="<?php print
$language->language ?>" lang="<?php print $language->language ?>"
dir="<?php print $language->dir ?>">
  <head>
    <title><?php print $head_title ?></title>
    <?php print $head ?>
    <?php print $styles ?>
    <style type="text/css" media="screen">
    #nav li.home a {background: #2266BB !important;color:
      #FFF !important}
    </style>
    <?php print $scripts ?>
  </head>
  <body>
<body id="">
<div id="wrapper">

<div id="main">

<div id="column">

<?php
        // Prepare header
        $site_fields = array();
        if ($site_name) {
          $site_fields[] = check_plain($site_name);
        }
        if ($site_slogan) {
          $site_fields[] = check_plain($site_slogan);
        }
```

```
    $site_title = implode(' ', $site_fields);
    if ($site_fields) {
        $site_fields[0] = '<span>'. $site_fields[0] .'</span>';
    }
    $site_html = implode(' ', $site_fields);

    if ($logo || $site_title) {
        print '<a href="'. check_url($front_page) .'" title="'.
            $site_title .'">';
        if ($logo) {
            print '<img src="'. check_url($logo) .'" alt="'.
                $site_title .'" id="logo" />';
        }
        print '</a>';
    }
?>
<div id="nav">
<?php if ($left): ?>
<?php if ($search_box): ?><div class="block"><?php print $search_box
?></div><?php endif; ?>
<?php print $left ?>
<?php endif; ?>
<div class="block">
<h2>Login</h2>
<p>block</p>
</div>
<ul>
<li class="home"><a rel="nofollow" href="#" title="">Home</a></li>
<li><a rel="nofollow" href="" title="">Menu</a></li>
<li><a rel="nofollow" href="" title="">Menu</a></li>
<li><a rel="nofollow" href="" title="">Menu</a></li>
<ul>
<li><a rel="nofollow" href="" title="">Menu</a></li>
<li><a rel="nofollow" href="" title="">Menu</a></li>
<li><a rel="nofollow" href="" title="">Menu</a></li>
</ul>
</li>
<li><a rel="nofollow" href="" title="">Menu</a></li>
<li><a rel="nofollow" href="" title="">Menu</a></li>
</ul>
<?php if ($right): ?>

        <?php if (!$left && $search_box): ?><div class="block">
            <?php print $search_box ?></div><?php endif; ?>
```

```
                    <?php print $right ?>
             <?php endif; ?>
  </div><!--/nav-->
  </div><!--/column-->

  <div id="main-content">
  <div id="header">

  </div><!--/header-->

  <div id="content">
   <?php if (isset($primary_links)) : ?>
            <?php print theme('links', $primary_links, array('class' =>
                   'links primary-links')) ?>
          <?php endif; ?>
          <?php if (isset($secondary_links)) : ?>
            <?php print theme('links', $secondary_links, array('class'
                   => 'links secondary-links')) ?>
          <?php endif; ?>
  <?php print $breadcrumb; ?>
            <?php if ($mission): print '<div id="mission">'.
                   $mission .'</div>'; endif; ?>
            <?php if ($tabs): print '<div id="tabs-wrapper"
                   class="clear-block">'; endif; ?>
            <?php if ($title): print '<h2'. ($tabs ? ' class=
                   "with-tabs"' : '') .'>'. $title .'</h2>'; endif; ?>
            <?php if ($tabs): print '<ul class="tabs primary">'.
                   $tabs .'</ul></div>'; endif; ?>
            <?php if ($tabs2): print '<ul class="tabs secondary">'.
                   $tabs2 .'</ul>'; endif; ?>
            <?php if ($show_messages && $messages): print $messages;
                   endif; ?>
            <?php print $help; ?>

              <?php print $content ?>

  </div><!--/content-->

  <div id="footer">
    <?php print $feed_icons ?>
  <?php print $footer_message . $footer ?>

  </div><!--/footer-->

  </div><!--/main-content-->

  <div class="clear"></div>
  </div><!--/main-->
```

```
</div><!--/wrapper-->

  <?php print $closure ?>
  </body>
</html>
```

When installed and viewed, this template appears as shown in the following screenshot:

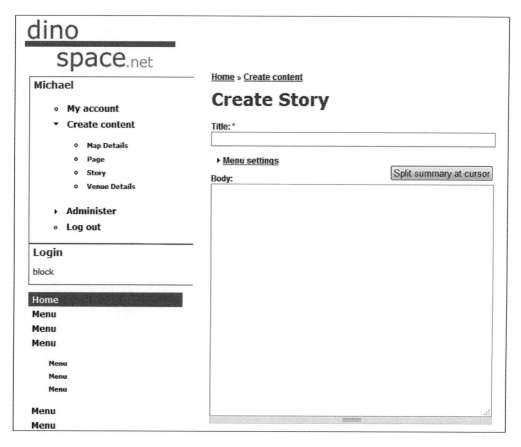

Obviously, there still remains a lot of work, but the basics seem to have been partially slotted into place. Some important points to be noted:

- The menu has automatically been placed in a div with a `block` class; the `block` style in our CSS was designed for blocks, and not the menu. To rectify this, we can change our CSS to rename `block` to `blockd` instead.

- The menu items have icons next to them. This is because Drupal includes a default stylesheet for the menus, which sets this. We will have to override this within our own CSS.

- Node, block and comment templates are still those from the default theme, although for this example, it isn't important.

- The default menu element is not selected. This is because the selected element in the page is given a CSS class of active; so we need to accommodate this in our CSS.

View source

One useful tip to remember is to view the source of the Drupal-generated page in your browser, and make a note of any style classes it gives to areas of the design, as these can be overridden by your own CSS.

To rectify these issues, the following additions to our CSS do the trick:

```
.active{ background: #2266BB !important;color: #FFF !important}
ul.menu { list-style-type: none !important; margin-left: 0px
!important;}
.blockd { margin-left: 25px; padding-left: 5px; border: 1px solid
#2266BB; }
.blockd h2 {color:#555; font-size: 120%;font-weight:bold; letter-
spacing:0; line-height:150%}
.block h2 {color:#555; font-size: 120%;font-weight:bold; letter-
spacing:0; line-height:150%}
.block ul{ list-style-image: none !important; list-style-type: none
!important; }
#block-user-0 {margin-left: 25px; padding-left: 5px; border: 1px solid
#2266BB; width: 210px; }
#block-user-0 ul {margin: 0px !important; padding:0px;}
#block-user-0 li {margin: 0px !important; list-style-type: none
!important; padding:0px;}
```

The #block-user-0 styles are for the login box, to make them fit in with the original design template we started with, as you will see further on in this chapter.

Template.php

As we discussed earlier, we are not using a `template.php` file in our theme.

Logo and screenshot

The logo in our site needs to be named `logo.png` for it to be automatically placed in by Drupal, so that if we were to distribute the theme, other administrators could change the logo by uploading a new one in the administration settings. A 150px by 90px image saved as `screenshot.png` serves as the screenshot.

In action

And there we have it, a very quick and basic theme of our own. With some time and thought we could customize the theme to any style we like. We've only scratched the surface with the themes we have created. There are of course many other areas of the theme which need to have proper attention paid to them, such as the breadcrumb trail, the primary or secondary menus (if used), blocks, forms, and messages (for instance when a new page is created).

When we are logged out, our log in box is nicely styled thanks to the other additions we've made to the CSS.

And of course, with the screenshot and various settings in the `.info` file, we have our theme listed nicely in **Administer | Site building | Themes**.

Summary

In this chapter, we looked at how to customize the look and feel of our site by:

- Enabling new themes
- Installing new themes
- Customizing themes
- Looking at the very basics of creating new themes

By customizing the look and feel of our site, we have given our social network a unique look to ensure the site is distinctive and stands out.

9
Deploying and Maintaining our Social Networking Site

Our new social networking web site is now complete, with one very important exception. It isn't online, which means nobody can join it, and it can't grow! Once we do put our site online, we need to keep our web site maintained too.

In this chapter, you will learn:

- How to keep your site secure
- How to protect your site from spam
- How to deploy your site
- How to maintain your site
- How to backup and restore your site

Installing the modules

As usual, let's install any module we will need during the chapter now, to save us time later. The modules we need are as follows and can be downloaded from the following:

- CAPTCHA—`http://www.drupal.org/project/captcha`
- reCAPTCHA—`http://drupal.org/project/recaptcha`
- Mollom—`http://drupal.org/project/mollom`
- Checkbox Validate—`http://drupal.org/project/checkbox_validate`
- Legal—`http://drupal.org/project/legal`

These need to be downloaded, extracted to our `modules` directory, and then enabled so that we can configure and use them later.

There are also some modules to look out for, as they are not currently available for Drupal 6. The Email verification module is one, which performs additional checks on email addresses entered when a user is registering to ensure that the address is valid. Another is the Login security module which provides protection from someone attempting to guess a user's password, including account locking, and delays to prevent such attempts from being successful. Other modules include the Flag content module and abuse modules.

Security

Our web site, once fully in use, will contain lots of personal information on our users, including their public profiles, their email addresses, and content they have contributed which may not be publicly viewable. We also have all the content on our site, which we want to keep secure. Essentially, security is important because we want to protect our web site and the data of our users.

Because Drupal is an open source project, with fully readable code, we have both additional protections and risks regarding security compared to other projects that are not open source. Since the code is readable, anyone can look through the code and potentially find security vulnerabilities. However, due to the nature of the Drupal community, it is also very easy to report bugs and security issues, and get them fixed and patched quickly: the community acts as a security auditor. Once an issue has been patched, we would then need to download the new release, and upgrade our installation, based on the upgrade documentation.

Security announcements

There is a section on the web site that is dedicated to security announcements, which makes it easy to keep up with the latest security patches released for the version of Drupal we are using. These security announcements are posted on this web site: `http://drupal.org/security`.

It is also advisable to subscribe to the mailing list for security announcements on this page, so that we can receive security announcements via email. This saves us from frequently checking this page for updates; alternatively, there is also an RSS feed for the content on this page which we could subscribe to.

Securing our site

So, what do the modules we installed do?

- reCAPTCHA—This module extends the CAPTCHA module and help prevent automated "web bots" from using and submitting forms, including registration forms, contact forms, and posting content.

- Mollom—This module comes into play in the unlikely event that an automated web bot is able to circumvent the CAPTCHA system. The mollom system checks whether the content submitted is SPAM. This can also prevent SPAM that is submitted by a genuine user, and can optionally fall back on a CAPTCHA system if it detects a SPAM posting.

- Legal module—This module adds a terms and conditions box to our sign up form, which users must read and accept before joining, informing them of the rules and policies of our site.

CAPTCHA

The **Completely Automated Public Turing test to tell Computers and Humans Apart (CAPTCHA)** module installs a test which proves you are human and prevents automated spam bots from signing up to our site.

The module allows us to set up one of three types of tests for use at various points throughout the site, including posting a comment, registering, and contacting a user. The three different tests, or challenges, available are:

- Math
- Image
- Text

Because we installed the reCAPTCHA module, we can also offer a reCAPTCHA-based test, which is seen as a large improvement over the Image test.

Let's have a look at an example for each of these different challenges.

Math

The math challenge involves a mathematical question, such as **1 + 0**, where the user must enter the answer in the appropriate text box.

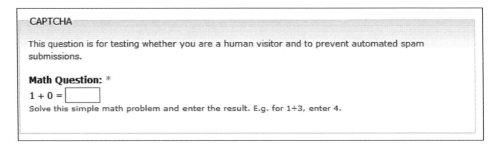

Image

The image challenge presents the user with an image containing various characters, the user has to read these characters and enter them correctly in a text box.

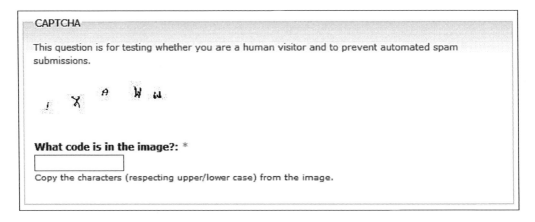

This challenge can be configured using the **Image CAPTCHA** tab in the CAPTCHA administration area. This allows us to set the font, the level of distortion in the background, and so on.

Text

The final test available by default is the text challenge, which asks for a portion of a phrase that is displayed to be entered correctly into a textbox.

CAPTCHA

This question is for testing whether you are a human visitor and to prevent automated spam submissions.

What is the fourth word in the phrase "apa xib qanay ohuhah rolahe"?: *

reCAPTCHA

The image CAPTCHA is the most effective test available. However, the quality of the images available with the module is very poor. reCAPTCHA is a very popular CAPTCHA service, and requires a little bit of configuration to get the set up done. We need to do the following:

- Download the reCAPTCHA library
- Sign up for an API key
- Enter the public and private keys provided to us

The configuration is described in the reCAPTCHA documentation page: `http://drupal.org/node/151588`.

Download the reCAPTCHA PHP library

If we go to the module configuration page (**Administer | User management | CAPTCHA**) and then click the **reCAPTCHA** tab, the following message appears at the top of the page: **The reCAPTCHA PHP library was not found. Please install it into sites/all/modules/recaptcha/recaptcha**.

To download the reCAPTCHA PHP library, we just need to click the link in that message, which then takes us to `http://recaptcha.net/plugins/php/index.html`. From here, we then simply click the **download** link. With the file downloaded, we simply need to extract the files into the `/sites/all/modules/recaptcha/recaptcha` folder.

Signup for an API key

Next, we need to click the **registered at reCAPTCHA.net** link on the reCAPTCHA module configuration page to sign up for our public and private keys. By clicking the link in the settings page, it passes over our web site address to prepopulate the **Create a reCAPTCHA key** form. The first stage is to register or log in to the reCAPTCHA web site, and then we are asked to create a key.

Because we have not deployed our site yet, the domain is populated with **localhost**. We can either accept this, and change the key to the value of our live domain later, when we deploy our site (as the key will only work with that domain), or we can check the **Enable this key on all domains (global key)** to ensure that it will work when we deploy the site, without any additional changes..

Once we have selected that, we need to click the **submit** button, and we are taken to a page containing a **Public** and **Private** key.

Enter our public and private keys

Next, we need to copy and paste these keys into the relevant text boxes on the **reCAPTCHA module configuration** page.

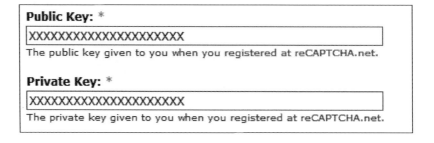

And then click the **Save configuration** button at the bottom of the page.

reCAPTCHA in action

If we now visit the examples page (**Administer | User management | CAPTCHA**), and then click the **Examples** subtab (`admin/user/captcha/captcha/examples`), we can see an example of this type of CAPTCHA test.

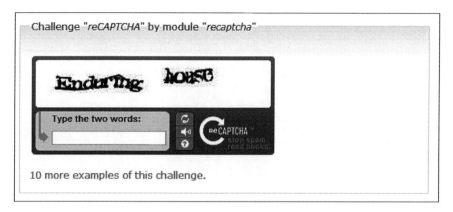

Now all that is left to do is set up the module so that the reCAPTCHA test is displayed to users at certain points on the site.

Setting it up

The module can be set up and configured from **Administer | User management | CAPTCHA**. Apart from setting up the module, we can also configure the image and text challenges via the tabs at the top of the page.

To enable the CAPTCHA challenges on certain forms, we just need to select the type of challenge we wish to enable for the relevant forms using the **Challenge type per form** option.

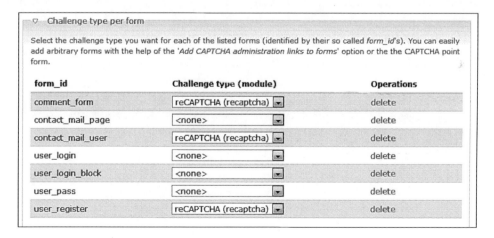

We can also set a short description that is displayed when a user is asked to complete a CAPTCHA challenge, perhaps to apologize for the inconvenience caused by the challenge, and explain why it is necessary for users to prove that they are genuine.

To prevent users from being continually pestered by the request to prove they are indeed human, we can alter the **Persistence** of the module to only challenge a user once, or to only challenge a user once for each type of form, and then not challenge them again.

Finally, we have the option to log the wrong responses. This is sent to the log within Drupal, and can be useful if we have users complaining that they cannot get through the CAPTCHA system.

Challenge description:

This question is for testing whether you are a human visitor

With this description you can explain the purpose of the challenge to the user.

Persistence:

○ Always add a challenge.

○ Omit challenges for a form once the user has successfully responded to a challenge for that form.

⦿ Omit challenges for all forms once the user has successfully responded to a challenge.

Define if challenges should be omitted during the rest of a session once the user successfully responses to a challenge.

☑ Log wrong responses

Report information about wrong responses to the log.

Mollom

Mollom provides two main services. It analyzes text to determine if the contents is SPAM, and it also offers CAPTCHA. If we wish, we can even use its CAPTCHA features in place of the CAPTCHA features set up with the reCAPTCHA and CAPTCHA modules.

Let's set up mollom to work alongside our current CAPTCHA setup, but with an additional backup of its own CAPTCHA system (in case it detects a SPAM posting). This works by sending certain form submissions such as a new page, comment or forum post, to the Mollom web service for analysis. If Mollom determines this to be a SPAM, the user is then asked to complete a CAPTCHA test.

As with reCAPTCHA, we need to sign up for public and private keys, as per the instructions mentioned on the **Administer | Site configuration | Mollom** page. These instructions contain links to the appropriate sign up page for Mollom.

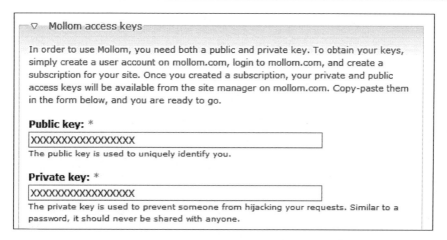

Once we have signed up, we need to enter the public and private keys into the appropriate boxes before clicking the **Save configuration** button.

The Mollom page then reloads, with a **Site usage statistics** section and **Spam protection settings**. The Site usage statistics section is an empty graph, which once our site starts making use of Mollom, will display a graph of spam attempts, and non-spam (ham) posts.

Since we have reCAPTCHA setup for the contact form pages, and registration forms, we should select the **No protection** option for these within Mollom. However, for content such as forum topics, book pages, and so on, we should use **Text analysis and CAPTCHA backup**.

Protect blog entry form:

Text analysis and CAPTCHA backup

Protect book page form:

Text analysis and CAPTCHA backup

Protect dinosaur friendly place form:

Text analysis and CAPTCHA backup

Protect forum topic form:

Text analysis and CAPTCHA backup

Protect map of dinosaur friendly places form:

Text analysis and CAPTCHA backup

Protect newsletter issue form:

Text analysis and CAPTCHA backup

Protect page form:

Text analysis and CAPTCHA backup

Legal

Under **Site configuration**, we now have a link to configure the **Legal** module. The options available for the module include:

- How the terms and conditions should be displayed; this can either be a scroll box of the content, some HTML text, or a separate page
- The **Terms & Conditions**
- Any additional checkboxes we wish to have (for instance, if we ran an over-18's social network, we could have a checkbox to indicate that the user is over 18)
- An explanation of changes made to the terms and conditions, which is displayed to users who signed up under a previous set of terms, so they know the new terms of the site

With terms and conditions in place, users are asked to accept them, as shown here:

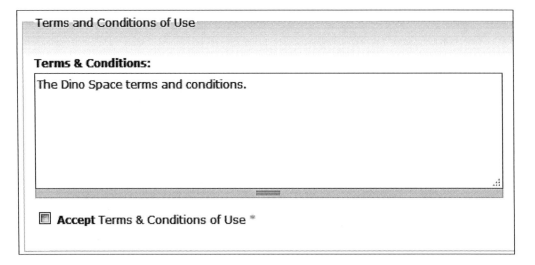

 This module is not yet compatible with the OpenID module.

Passwords

As the web site owner, our passwords can provide access to the administration area of the web site. Our hosting account password also gives complete access to our web site (even elements which may not be powered by Drupal), databases, emails, and statistics; so it is important that we use secure passwords.

Passwords which are not secure can be obtained by random guesses, automated dictionary attacks where a computer goes through a list of words trying them as the password, or through social engineering. Unfortunately, the Login security module is not yet available for Drupal 6. This module would provide an additional layer of protection from this form of attack, by locking accounts after a number of incorrect login attempts; so do keep an eye out for the progress of that module, and other similar modules.

Strong passwords are generally difficult to guess. Here are some suggestions for creating a strong password:

- Use both letters and numbers.
- Make use of special characters such as @, /, \, #, *, and so on.
- Make all of your passwords unique. If the passwords are the same for every login, guessing your Drupal password will enable access to your personal email, other web sites you are a member of, and so on.
- Include spelling mistakes, to make the word harder to guess.
- Don't include personal information such as date of birth, names of family members, and so on.
- Consider using numbers in place of some letters.

Deploying

To put our web site online, we need to do the following:

- Register a domain name, for example, www.dinospace.net
- Set up a hosting account
- Create a database on the hosting account
- Upload our database to the hosting account
- Upload our site to the hosting account
- Tweak the settings to point to the new database

Hosting and domain names

There are many hosting providers and domain name registrars available, and as such, prices are generally quite competitive.

When looking for a web host, it is important to keep in mind the amount of web space required, bandwidth (amount of data that can be transferred from your web site to your users per month), service level agreement, minimum contract term, acceptable usage policy and of course the cost.

Most hosting accounts come with access to a web-based control panel to make many administrative matters easy, such as setting up email accounts, creating databases and so on. cPanel and Plesk are two of the most common control panels available. This chapter assumes that you have a hosting account with cPanel, although the instructions can easily be adapted to any control panel. If you would like more information and help with the cPanel hosting control panel, you may find *cPanel User Guide and Tutorial* by Aric Pedersen ISBN 978-1-904811-92-3, published by Packt Publishing (www.packtpub.com/cPanel/book), useful.

 www.webhostingtalk.com is a popular forum discussing web hosts, and comparing different hosting companies. It may prove useful when choosing a hosting account.

Some popular web hosting providers include:

- 1&1 Internet Inc (www.1and1.co.uk)
- A Small Orange (www.asmallorange.com)
- Site5 (www.site5.com)
- MediaTemple (www.mediatemple.net)

The domain name is the address which points to the hosting account (for example, www.dougsdinos.com). Because of competitive prices you shouldn't expect to pay more than USD$10 per year for a domain name. Some popular domain name registrars include:

- NameCheap (www.namecheap.com)
- GoDaddy (www.godaddy.com)

Once you have registered a domain name, you will need to point it to your web hosting account by changing its nameservers to those of the hosting accounts. Your host should be able to provide information on the nameservers you will need to use, and your domain name registrar should be able to provide information on updating your domain nameservers.

Getting the site online

Now that we have a registered domain name and a hosting account, we can put our social networking site online. To do this, we need to:

- Create a user account for the database
- Create a new database
- Assign the user account permissions to that database
- Upload our site
- Import the database
- Updating a setting to tell the site to use the database on the hosting account

Uploading Files

To upload the files to our web hosting account, we need an FTP client. There are a number of products available that are both free and commercial. I would recommend using FileZilla (http://filezilla-project.org/) for this purpose.

Setting up the database

Firstly, we need to log in to our control panel (this is usually www.yourdomain.com/cpanel), find the **Databases** section, and click the **MySQL Database Wizard** icon.

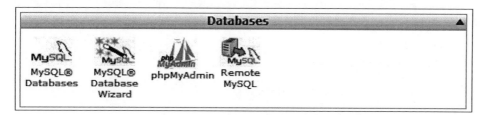

The first stage is to enter a name for the new database. Normally, this is combined with the hosting accounts usernames, so the database name dinos would become dinospac_dinos. Once we have entered a name, we need to click **Next Step**, to move on to the next stage of the database wizard.

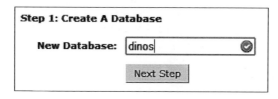

Next, we need to create a MySQL user which will connect to the database server to access the database we have just created. It is important to use a secure password, we can use the **Generate Password** button to have cPanel automatically generate a secure password for us.

Once we have done that, we need to click the **Next Step** button.

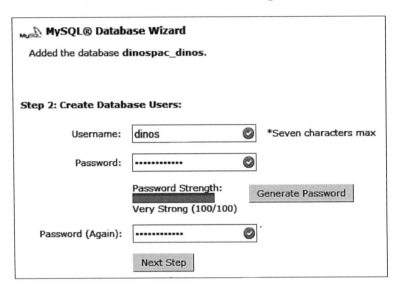

Now that we have a database and a database user, we need to grant permissions for that user to be able to manage the database. Let's check the **ALL PRIVILEGES** checkbox and click the **Next Step** button again.

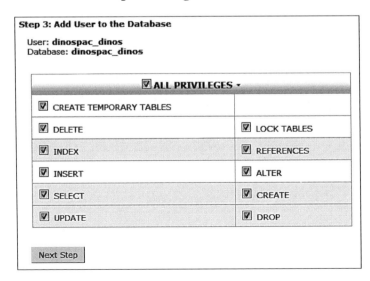

We now have a database, and a **Username** and **Password** to connect to the database. The next stage is to import the database from our local installation to the database on our web hosting account.

Importing the local database

This is a two step process. Firstly, we need to export the local database, and then we need to import it into the database in our web hosting account.

The database can be exported from our local phpMyAdmin installation (comes included with most local web server setups, for example, WAMPServer). We need to open `http://localhost/phpmyadmin/` in a web browser. From here, we need to select the **Database** we are using from the drop-down list.

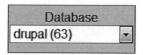

With the database selected, the page should reload the display of a number of tabs across the top of the screen, and a list of tables in the database in the main area of the window. We need to click the **Export** tab at the top.

From here, we need to ensure that all the tables are selected (we can click **Select All** to make sure they are), scroll to the bottom of the page, and check the **Save as file** box, before clicking **Go** which will prompt us to download the database export.

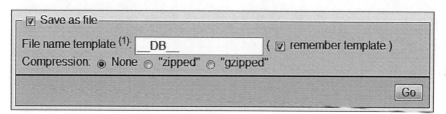

Now that we have the database from our local installation saved, we can import it into the database on our web hosting account. From our **cPanel** control panel, we need to click the **phpMyAdmin** link.

If we have more than one database setup, we need to select it from the list (as we did with our local version). If not, we just need to click the database from the left hand pane.

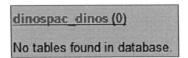

Next, we need to select the **Import** tab from the top of the window, so that we can import the database.

From this window, we can browse for the database file on our computer using the **Choose File** button and then clicking the **Go** button at the bottom of the page.

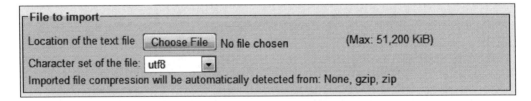

We now have our database setup on our hosting account!

Uploading the site

The next stage is to upload our site onto our web hosting account. To do this, we need an FTP client, such as FileZilla.

We need to enter our domain name, web hosting account **Username** and **Password** into the relevant boxes, and then click **Quickconnect**.

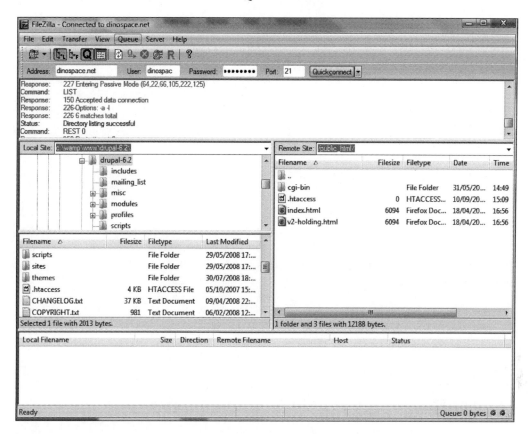

Once we are connected with our FTP client, we need to navigate to the `public_html/` folder in the **Remote Site** pane (this may be `htdocs`, or something similar depending on the hosting control panel you use). In the **Local Site** pane, we need to navigate to our Drupal folder, simply select all the files, and drag them into the **Remote Site** pane to upload them to our web hosting account.

Changing the database settings

With the web site and database uploaded, we now need to update the settings file in our Drupal installation to point to the database on the hosting account. The database connection details are located in the `settings.php` file (in the `sites/default` folder). We need to download this file, and open it with a text editor (or a PHP editor such as the Crimson editor).

```
88  * Database URL format:
89  *    $db_url = 'mysql://username:password@localhost/databasename';
90  *    $db_url = 'mysqli://username:password@localhost/databasename';
91  *    $db_url = 'pgsql://username:password@localhost/databasename';
92  */
93 $db_url = 'mysqli://root@localhost/drupal';
94 $db_prefix = '';
```

Within this file, we need to find the line starting with `$db_url`, and update this line to contain the database name, username, and password that we set up in our hosting account. This needs to be in the following format: `mysqli://database_user:database_password@localhost/database_name`.

Once we have updated this, we need to re-upload the file, and our web site is now accessible via the Internet!

Maintenance

From time to time, we may wish to perform some maintenance on our site. Let's look at three common ways of maintaining our installation.

- Automated maintenance—Cron
- Making changes and updating our site
- Analyzing Drupal reports and performing maintenance accordingly

Cron

Cron is the automated execution of tasks by our server. Many of Drupal modules perform regular maintenance tasks (for example, pruning log files). By using cron, these tasks can be automatically performed at specific intervals.

Setting up cron jobs is quite technical, and also depends on your hosting provider, as not all hosting providers allow cron jobs to be run. You should contact your web host for more information on setting up a cron job.

The Drupal handbook online contains more information about setting up cron.
`http://drupal.org/cron`.

Performing maintenance

When we decide to make some major changes to our site, it would be a good idea
to put the site into maintenance mode. This prevents other users from accessing the
site at a time when they are more likely to experience errors resulting from changes
being made while they are browsing the site.

There is a maintenance option within Drupal specifically for this purpose. It turns the
web site offline to our users, and displays our message. This option is found under
Administer | Site configuration | Site maintenance.

From here, we just need to select the **Site status** as **Off-line**, and enter a **Site off-line
message** to be displayed to users trying to access the site.

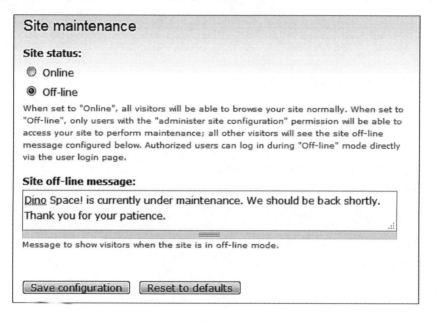

If we now go back to the homepage of the site, there is a message there to remind us
(as an administrator) that the website is in offline mode, and our users won't be able
to access the site.

If we logout, we can see that the site is inaccessible, and we are presented with the message we set earlier.

Logging into an offline site

To log back into the site, we need to go directly to the user page, which will prompt us to login, for example, `www.dinospace.net/user/` (`?q=user` if Nice URL's not enabled).

Upgrading Drupal

When new versions of Drupal are released, we may wish to upgrade to a newer version, especially if it is a new security release. Upgrading is quite a straightforward process. However, one thing we do need to be careful about is our modules. If we upgraded to a new major release of Drupal (for example, Drupal 7) we would probably find that most of our modules would not work. When new releases are available, with security updates, a message is displayed in the administration panel. Although the upgrade process may vary from upgrade to upgrade, the process generally involves:

- Downloading the new version of Drupal
- Backing up your web site
- Backing up your database
- Uploading the files from the new version to the site
- Visiting our site and accessing the `update.php` file to make any necessary database changes

Of course, full detailed documentation is provided within each upgrade.

Reports

Drupal provides us with a number of reports in the administration area, which can advise us on the areas where maintenance may be required. These reports include:

- Recent log entries of various events that have been recorded, including users logging in, email problems, and actions relating to content
- Top "access denied" errors listing attempts by users to access content they are not permitted to see

- Top "page not found" errors listing the top access attempts to pages which don't exist on our site

- Available updates that list updates which are available for our modules and themes

- Status report which checks for problems with our site, for example, whether cron is setup

How can these help?

If we are finding a lot of access denied errors, then we are likely to have a link in a menu or page (which most of our users can see) to pages they shouldn't have access to. We should then look for this link and remove it. Similarly, if we are having a lot of "page not found" errors for certain pages, then we may have a link to a page which does not exist, and we should remove the link. Alternatively, it may be due to a page we removed. We could set up a redirect to a replacement page, or put up a page explaining why the page was removed.

The available updates report can help us keep our modules up-to-date. While upgrading modules and themes, it is advisable to put the web site into maintenance mode, to prevent our users experiencing any errors.

Backing up

Taking regular backups of your site is important in case something were to happen to the web site, its hosting account, or even the server the web site is stored on. If we were to lose several weeks worth of community contributions, this could do some serious damage to our community.

 It is also worth checking backup procedures your web host may perform, as part of your service.

The frequency of contributions and how active the site really is determine how frequently we need to backup. Initially, a weekly backup would probably be sufficient. However, as the site gets more active, we may wish to automate the process on a nightly basis.

Backing up with cPanel

From the main cPanel interface in the **Files** section, there is a link to the **Backups** area.

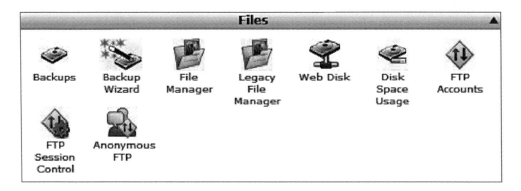

From here we can download a copy of our **Home Directory** (all of the files and most of our settings) and also a copy of the database. Clicking the relevant backup buttons will prompt us to download the backup files immediately.

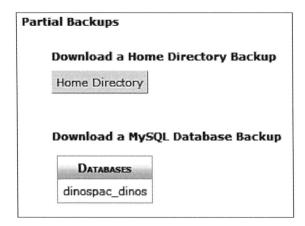

It is important to keep these files stored in place that is safe and secure.

Restoring

Backups are needed in case we have a problem and lose our data. However, if this does happen, we need to be able to restore our web site from the backups. Let's look at the restore process within cPanel.

Restoring within cPanel

When logged into cPanel, we need to click the **Backups** button to go to the backups section, as we did when backing up the site.

On the right hand side of this screen are the options to **Restore a Home Directory Backup** and to **Restore a MySQL Database**.

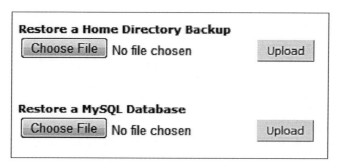

To restore from the backups, all we need to do is browse for the file we wish to restore from, and then click **Upload**.

Any existing database or home directory content will be removed; so do this only if you really need to. If you need to gain access to a specific file which you need to backup, decompress the home directory backup, look for the file and upload it to your site using an FTP client.

Summary

In this chapter, we looked at how to deploy our social networking site on the Internet, and how to maintain it using the maintenance mode, reports, and cron, and to keep everything running smoothly. We also looked into keeping backups of our site in case anything went wrong, and how to restore from a backup if we needed to. Hopefully, we won't need to use the restore feature. But it is important to know how to use it in case we needed to.

10
Promoting our Site

We now have our social networking site up and running, and it is live on the Internet. However, without users viewing the web site, making contributions, and communicating with each other via the web site, our social network won't be successful. Bringing new users to our site is key to help it grow. So let's now look at how we can promote our web site!

In this chapter, you will learn:

- About advertising your social network with ad space, pay per click ads, and newsletter ads
- How to avoid being penalized by search engines
- About social and viral marketing
- How to optimize your social network for search engines

Online advertising

On the Internet, there are many different advertising programs available, including:

- Simply purchasing advertisement space
- Professional advertisement networks
- Search engine advertisements
- Newsletter advertising

Typically, both professional advertisement networks and search engine advertisements (that is sponsored links in search results and on-site advertisements provided by search engines) operate on a **PPC** (**pay per click**) basis, where you pay each time a user clicks on your advertisement and goes to your site.

Buying advertisement space

Some web sites sell advertisement space, which can in some cases be a great way of generating new traffic, and bringing new users to a site. There are a few things to bear in mind when buying advertisement space on a web site, which are:

- Competition—Is the web site you are going to advertise on a competitor, or does the site compete in some way with yours? If it is a competitor, then it isn't the best place to advertise, nor is the site likely to accept your ad. We certainly shouldn't advertise our Dino Space site on sites such as Dino Spaces, Dino Community and other potential competitors.

- Relevancy—We wouldn't gain anything by advertising on a web site which isn't relevant. If it isn't relevant, then the visitors would have no desire to click the ad and come to our site. After all, visitors to an office supply store web site wouldn't be interested in participating in an online dinosaur pet owner community!

- Reputation—If the site you are advertising on isn't reputed, then you are not likely to get many visitors and you are also associating your site with one which is not reputable. Do some research and investigation on the web site first.

- Statistics—A relevant, non-competing and reputed web site isn't enough! The popularity of the web site you are advertising on is also important, especially if it is a paid advertisement. Web sites with a low number of visitors won't bring many visitors to your site; so make sure you know a bit about their statistics, or make sure you pay for a certain number of impressions on the site.

Pay Per Click Advertisements

With Pay Per Click (PPC) advertisements, as the name implies, you pay only when a visitor clicks on your ad and visits your web site. This is often seen as a better option than just paying for advertising space, because you pay only when you get a new visitor. With many of these services, you pay in advance, and can set daily and monthly budgets. Let's take a look at how PPC advertising generally works:

- First, we sign up with a network (see the next section for a few networks provided by search engines).

- We submit information about the web site, ourselves, and some billing information.

- We select keywords we wish to target, such as dinosaurs, pet dinosaurs, caring for dinosaurs, dinosaur community and so on. These are keywords which a user might type into a search engine; or if the ad is shown on a web site, these may be the keywords on the site.

- Select a maximum amount to pay for each click (sometimes, this affects the position and frequency of display of our advert) as well as a daily and monthly budget.

The monthly budgets mean that if we choose not to prepay, but to link a credit card to the advertisement network instead, our bill would not exceed the specified budget.

 Advertisers are often concerned about fraudulent clicks; a competitor could repeatedly click our advert, bringing in no genuine new visitors but costing us money! Thankfully, most advertisement networks have systems in place to detect this. Make sure you know if the advertisement network you sign up for has appropriate detection for fraudulent clicks, so you don't waste your marketing budget!

Advertisement networks provided by search engines

The following are links to some advertisement networks provided by three major search engines, which are reputed and used by thousands of people for advertising their web sites:

- Google (`http://www.google.co.uk/intl/en/ads/`)
- Yahoo! (`http://sem.smallbusiness.yahoo.com/searchenginemarketing/index.php`)
- Microsoft (`http://advertising.microsoft.com/search-advertising?s_int=277`)

Some of these networks allow both text and image ads, but generally, image ads are shown only in large ad units (when a web site owner opts to display ads on their site; they choose which size of ad-unit they wish to display. Large units typically consist of between four and six standard ads), and can be costly as such.

The future for PPC: Pay Per Action

Some advertisement networks are starting to implement pay per action schemes, where instead of paying per click, you pay every time a user who clicked your advert completes a specific action. This could include signing up, or making a contribution (ideal for our site), or making a purchase.

Newsletter advertising

Similar to advertising on relevant web sites, we could advertise our social network on relevant email newsletters. Maybe there is a local dinosaur related organization which has an email bulletin. Advertising in such newsletters could help bring new visitors to the site.

There are also a number of web sites that are dedicated to help you manage an advertisement campaign within email newsletters.

Caution: Search Engine Penalization

Most search engines use a number of different metrics to determine where a web site is positioned in a list of search results. Some search engines, such as Google have a metric (Google's is called Page Rank which factors in other things too) which is based on in-bound links, where a web site link from one site to another acts as a vote.

Some web sites and businesses use this to their advantage, and offer to pay for advertising space on other web sites (normally ones which have a high ranking). Both the buying and selling of advertising in this way is not something which many search engines like. Google even has an online tool to report web sites that do this, which result in their rankings being penalized.

Of course, there is nothing wrong with buying and selling advertising space. In fact, one of Google's core businesses revolves around advertising space. The solution is to alter how the link is structured.

A traditional link is structured as follows:

```
<a href='http://www.packtpub.com'>PacktPub</a>
```

If this was a paid advert on our site (or if we were buying the advert space on a site) we could structure the link like this:

```
<a href='http://www.packtpub.com' rel='nofollow'>PacktPub</a>
```

The `nofollow` attribute signals to search engines that we don't wish the link to be counted as a vote for the web sites rankings. So if this was an advertisement, we would not be penalized by search engines for buying or selling advertising space for it, on a web site.

 It is important to note that there is nothing wrong with providing links to other web sites without the `rel=nofollow` attribute. The penalty is applicable only to those adverts which are bought or sold, but not containing this attribute, as this is considered a trick to fool the rankings.

Things to keep in mind:

- Only purchase ads, or buy ads from reputed web sites. Don't buy or sell links.

- **Always** use `rel='nofollow'` for the adverts you are displaying on your web site which you are paid to display, and for adverts you have on other web sites.

- Beware of emails offering to pay to put adverts on your web site–they probably don't have the `rel='nofollow'` attribute.

- Don't risk your search engine rankings!

Newsletters

We have already spent some time looking at Newsletters. However, it is important to remember that they are a very important marketing tool, not just for reminding existing members about the site, but for collecting the email addresses of new users to the site, so we can email them and entice them back!

Marketing materials

Physical marketing materials are a fantastic way to promote a new web site. Unfortunately they have high costs associated with them; so with a low budget your target would be limited to a small geographical area.

Starting with something simple and low cost such as business cards could help, not to act as business cards, but as mini ads. These could contain information about our social network, as well as its web address. They are great for distributing at relevant events, such as dinosaur conventions, or if you happen to be talking to someone who would have an interest in the site (perhaps someone who is having difficulty in bathing their T-Rex!).

Social marketing

We can use other (non-competing, obviously!) social networks to help promote our network, as most social networking web sites have provisions for user information and profile data, including web site addresses. We can add our URL to MySpace profiles, Facebook profiles, Twitter accounts, and so on, to try and provide that extra promotion to our site.

Facebook has a new addition to its web site which allows business, bands, web sites, organizations and anything that isn't related to a personal profile to create their own page, providing additional information, as well as hosting a discussion forum, photo gallery, and other features. We can of course create a profile for our site and share it among our friends. Users of Facebook can also become fans of these pages, promoting the site among their own friends as well.

Viral marketing

Viral Marketing is a relatively new marketing concept, which revolves around utilizing social networks. One particular example of viral marketing is utilizing video sharing web sites such as YouTube, and promoting videos that advertise businesses, web sites, products or services by using them in the video. This technique is probably more suited to large social networking sites with large marketing budgets who are trying to promote a brand. Information on using YouTube in particular was recently posted on a technology blog called TechCrunch (`http://www.techcrunch.com/2007/11/22/the-secret-strategies-behind-many-viral-videos/`).

Twitter

Twitter (`http://www.twitter.com/`) is a social networking web site revolving around the concept of telling your followers / anyone who is interested, what you are doing at a particular moment, as you may remember from Chapter 6, *Communicating with our Users*. In Chapter 6, we focused on adding a Twitter feed to our site to provide mini-updates directly from the site. However, we can use it to bring in new members. If you have your own Twitter account, you can update your followers to changes or announcements related to your web site. One option is to create a Twitter account specifically for the Dino Space site, and use it to post information about the Dino Space site periodically. Existing members of the web site may be interested in "following" the Twitter account, making it easier for others to find our Twitter account, and subsequently our site!

Twitter has recently added a new search feature, allowing you to search for specific keywords—a great way to track discussion of your site across the "twitterverse"!

Social bookmarking

Social bookmarking is a web-based method for storing and managing bookmarks. Sites such as dig, `StumbleUpon.com` and `del.icio.us` are examples of social bookmarking sites. When a user adds a site to their social bookmarking service, it is easier for others who use that service to find it. If they enjoy the link, it will be promoted, and will gain even more exposure. We can add social bookmarking links to the footer of every page in our site, which allows the user to submit pages to these social bookmarking services, and also help us improve our marketing.

As there are a lot of different services, it is a good idea to make use of a service that allows users to send the links to the social bookmarking service of their choice. One example of such as service is **Socializer** (`http://ekstreme.com/socializer/`). This provides more information on the service, as well as some PHP code which we could add to our web site's footer for displaying the socialize link. Now if a user wants to share the link with others, they simply click the **Socialize** link and select the service they use. It may also be worthwhile to add a link to "share on Facebook" as that is not available with the Socializer service. A module has been created for a similar service, called AddThis (`http://drupal.org/project/addthis`).

The Digg Effect/ Slashdot effect

One thing to be aware of is the so called Digg effect/Slashdot effect. If a site submitted to services such as Digg is found to be popular, it can send a very large amount of traffic to the site, which can cause problems, if you are using a shared hosting environment. You may wish to discuss provisions for this with your hosting supplier.

Search Engine Optimization

Search Engine Optimization (SEO) can be a real traffic booster, as it makes our site more visible to search engines, easier for them to read, and makes our site seem more important and more relevant.

There are two main aspects to Search Engine Optimization: on-site and off-site.

On-site SEO

On-site search engine optimization relates to making optimizations directly on the web site. This improves visibility and readability to search engines.

Meta

Meta tags are tags stored in the head section of an HTML document, typically for information on keywords, description, and the author of the web site.

This is not regarded very highly by search engines anymore, but it is still worth doing, particularly if different pages and sections have different meta data.

There is a module which enables Meta tags to be set on a per node basis available at `http://drupal.org/project/nodewords`.

Sitemap and webmaster tools

Google has released some webmaster tools, including one that allows us to create a list of the pages within our site, rank them in the order of importance and specify the frequency in which those sections will be updated. This is then saved as an XML file and stored on the web site. Google can then read it and see which content it should check regularly, and which content it should check less regularly. This helps keep the web site more relevant to search engines.

A module has been written to automatically create sitemaps. However, the Drupal 6 version is still under development; it is certainly worth keeping an eye on (`http://drupal.org/project/xmlsitemap`).

Links

A very simple trick is to make use of relevant keywords within sentences as hyperlinks and give them relevant title attributes, take the example of a products page. A poorly optimized link would be:

```
To view our dinosaur care tips <a href="dinosaurcaretips/">click
here</a>.
```

The link has no context and no meaningful information, a more meaningful and search engine friendly link would be:

```
Why not view our <a href="dinosaur-care-tips/" title="View our
Dinosaur Care Tips | Dino Space">dinosaur care tips</a>
```

All these small changes do make a difference!

Up-to-date content

Keep content up-to-date! If the content on our web site is always the same, with rare changes made to it, search engines (and visitors!) will stop crawling the web site. Frequent updates make the search engines pay more attention to your site.

Off-site SEO

Off-site search engine optimization is particularly useful for specific key words to obtain certain specified rankings in search engines. It relies on promoting the web site on other web sites; hence it is called off-site SEO.

As we had discussed earlier, one of the metrics for a web site's position in search results are its inbound links. Commenting on web sites, blogs, forums, video posts, profiles and so on with web links can increase a web site's ranking. This should always be done with care, consideration and courtesy, for instance, with a link in your personal signature on forums. Spamming web sites with comments is a very bad practice. However, relevant and appropriate comments on relevant web sites and articles, with a link back to our site, is a good start. Many companies specialize in this form of SEO. So if it is something you are serious about, it is worth looking around to see what they can offer.

Monetizing your site

The other important consideration is to monetize your site. While your site may not be designed to make a profit, it may be useful to try and recuperate expenses such as hosting fees. Here are some simple options to get you started:

- Cafepress.com—Creates merchandise with your sites logo, and earns a percentage from the sales; this could be prominently promoted on the site

- Google AdSense—Advertisement blocks from Google on the site earn money on a per-click basis; alternatively, integrating a Google search feature provides a less obtrusive form of advertising

- Affiliate Marketing—Become an affiliate of sites such as Amazon, where relevant products can be promoted on the site, and a commission earned

Summary

In this chapter, we have looked at promoting our web site on the Internet using advertisements, advertising networks, other social networks and search engine optimization. Now you have your social network up and running, and you have some advice for promoting and marketing your social network—it is up to you to make it successful. Good luck!

Installing WAMP

In order to install Drupal and the various social networking modules on our own computer, we need a development environment to run it that includes:

- A web server
- PHP
- A database server (MySQL)
- Various PHP and web server libraries to utilize additional features

WampServer is a package providing all of these, and more, for Microsoft Windows systems. Mac users may wish to take a look at **MAMP** (Macintosh, Apache, MySQL and PHP) at `http://www.mamp.info/en/mamp/index.html`, while Linux users will need to look for instructions for setting up **LAMP** (Linux, Apache, MySQL and PHP) on their particular distribution.

Installing WampServer

Now we know what we need to install; so let's get started!

Downloading WampServer

Firstly, we need to download the software from the Internet. WampServer is available at `http://www.wampserver.com/en/download.php`. From here, we click the **DOWNLOAD WampServer 2.0** link which then takes us to **SourceForge** from where we download the web site.

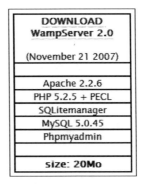

Installing WampServer

Once downloaded, we need to install the software. First, let's open the file we have just downloaded. We may need to agree to some security dialogues before Windows allows us to install the software.

 You must be logged in as an administrator to install WampServer.

The first window to be displayed warns us that we shouldn't try to upgrade from a previous version of WampServer and that we need to uninstall the older versions if any. Now, let's click on **Yes** so that the installation can continue.

Next, we are presented with the installation splash screen; here, we need to click **Next**.

Then we need to select the **I accept the agreement** button before clicking the **Next** button.

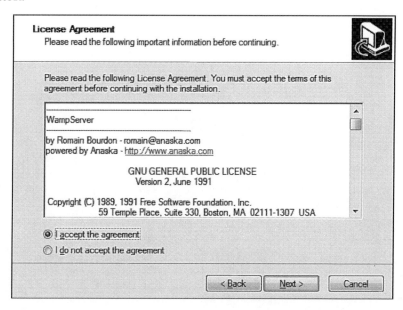

Now, we need to select the location where we wish to install WampServer. If we are happy with the default location, we should click **Next**; otherwise, we should change the location first.

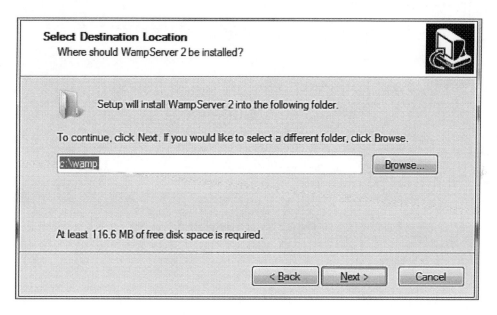

If we wish to add shortcuts to WampServer to our desktop, or to the Quicklaunch toolbar, we can do so by selecting the appropriate checkboxes before clicking **Next**.

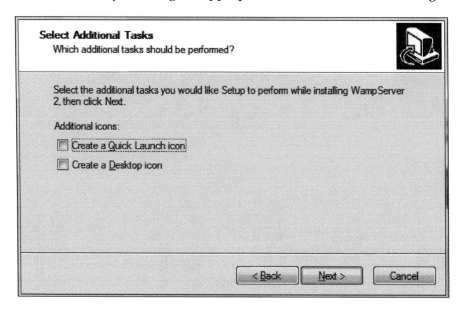

Before WampServer is actually installed, we are shown an overview of the options we have selected. We can click **Install** provided everything is fine, otherwise we need to click **Back** and make the changes if any.

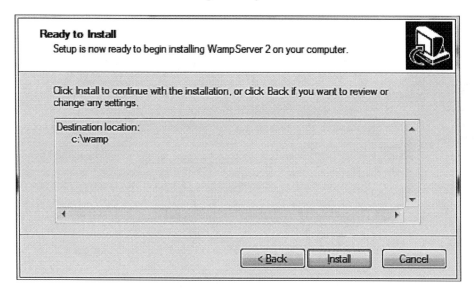

WampServer will then install onto our computer.

Once the installation has completed, we are asked to confirm our primary web browser. By default, it selects the Windows Internet Explorer; if we are happy with that, we should click **Open**, otherwise we should look for an alternative browser. Next, the installation asks for the details for sending mails from PHP. On most installations, we won't be able to send mails from PHP scripts because we have no mail server installed; so just click **Next**.

We now have WampServer installed; if we click **Finish** WampServer will start.

Apache not starting?

If WampServer doesn't start (the icon in the system tray will show red or orange) it may mean that something else is utilizing the computer port (Apache runs on (port 80) and programs such as Skype do this). So you may need to close other applications before trying to start WampServer.

WampServer overview

When WampServer is running, it is displayed in our computer's system tray alongside the clock. Clicking the icon displays a menu where we can configure our server, and start or stop various services.

Putting the server online would make the web pages on our computer accessible to other computers on our network, and potentially via the Internet. We can quickly start, stop and restart the services, configure each of them, open the folder containing our web site's files, and open our web site or database manager in a web browser.

Configuring WampServer

Within the WampServer menu, the Apache, PHP, and MySQL options allow us to configure the various services. We can install modules and add-ons to the different components, or we can edit the configuration files for them.

There are the two main features that we will want to be enabled:

- GD for PHP
- Rewrite_module for Apache

Configuration Files

The `my.ini`, `php.ini`, and `httpd.conf` files are the configuration files for the three services, although we wouldn't need to edit these for our web site. However, it is important to know where they are, in case we do need to change them later, as they control how the software works. More information is available on their respective web sites.

GD2

PHP's GD2 module is a graphics library that allows PHP to easily manipulate and manage images, including resizing images, recreating images, adding watermarks to images and so on. Drupal has a number of image features which require an image module to be installed with PHP. By default, GD2 is installed with WampServer; but it is important for us to confirm that it is enabled, and that we know where the setting is.

PHP's modules are enabled and disabled by clicking the WampServer logo in the system tray selecting **PHP** and then the **PHP Extensions**.

From here, we can enable or disable the GD2 extension.

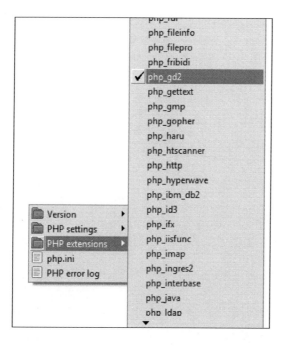

Rewrite Module

Apache has a module called **rewrite** which allows it to rewrite URLs, particularly to make them more friendly by rewriting URLs such as /home/about to index.php?s ection=home&page=about. Now, when a user types in the "clean URL" version, the web site interoperates this properly.

Drupal's Clean URL's module makes use of this feature if it is available; so let's enable it! It can be enabled from **Apache modules** within the **Apache** menu.

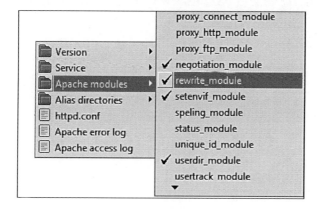

Summary

We have now installed the Apache web server, the PHP interpreter and MySQL database server using the WampServer package. We have also ensured that various options are enabled which Drupal will utilize later on for our social networking site.

Index

N

newsletters, Drupal site 269
nodes 36
non core module. *See* FeedAPI module
notifications module 140

O

off-site SEO 273
on-site SEO
  links 272
  meta tags 272
  sitemap tools 272
  up-to-date content 272
  webmaster tools 272
online advertising, Drupal site
  about 265
  advertisement networks, by search engines
      267
  advertising space buying, guidelines 266
  newsletter advertising 268
  Pay Per Click (PPC) advertisements
      266, 267
  Pay Per Click (PPC) advertisements,
      future 268
  search engine penalization 268, 269
OpenID
  logging in, with 136, 137
  user already exists 137
  user does not exists 137
OpenID module 110, 136
organic groups module
  about 169
  block, enabling 171, 172
  configuring 169
  group, creating 172, 173
  group, using 173, 174
  group content type, creating 170
  page content type, configuring 171

P

permissions 117
PHPList 181
polls, Drupal modules
  about 89

creating 90
roles 92
pre-installed themes, Drupal
  bluemarine 217
  chameleon 218
  garland 218, 219
  marvin 219
  minnelli 219
  pushbutton 220
profile module
  about 118
  fields 118
  fields, adding to site 118
  overview 119
  user profile, extending 119

R

reCAPTCHA
  about 245
  API key signing up for 246
  private keys entering 246
  public keys entering 246
  reCAPTCHA PHP library, downloading
      245
relationships, Drupal site
  building, between users 141
  creating 142
  default relationship 148
  my relationships page 150
  permissions 147
  planning 141
  relationship, creating with other user
      148, 149
  settings 145
reports, Drupal administation
  access denied, errors 60
  available updates 60
  final status report 61
  page not found, errors 60
  recent log entries 60
rewrite module 281
roles
  about 105, 117
  additonal roles, creating 106
  anonymous role permissions 105, 117
  anonymous user roles 105, 117

Thank you for buying
Drupal 6 Social Networking

Packt Open Source Project Royalties

When we sell a book written on an Open Source project, we pay a royalty directly to that project. Therefore by purchasing Drupal 6 Social Networking, Packt will have given some of the money received to the Drupal project.

In the long term, we see ourselves and you—customers and readers of our books—as part of the Open Source ecosystem, providing sustainable revenue for the projects we publish on. Our aim at Packt is to establish publishing royalties as an essential part of the service and support a business model that sustains Open Source.

If you're working with an Open Source project that you would like us to publish on, and subsequently pay royalties to, please get in touch with us.

Writing for Packt

We welcome all inquiries from people who are interested in authoring. Book proposals should be sent to author@packtpub.com. If your book idea is still at an early stage and you would like to discuss it first before writing a formal book proposal, contact us; one of our commissioning editors will get in touch with you.

We're not just looking for published authors; if you have strong technical skills but no writing experience, our experienced editors can help you develop a writing career, or simply get some additional reward for your expertise.

About Packt Publishing

Packt, pronounced 'packed', published its first book "Mastering phpMyAdmin for Effective MySQL Management" in April 2004 and subsequently continued to specialize in publishing highly focused books on specific technologies and solutions.

Our books and publications share the experiences of your fellow IT professionals in adapting and customizing today's systems, applications, and frameworks. Our solution-based books give you the knowledge and power to customize the software and technologies you're using to get the job done. Packt books are more specific and less general than the IT books you have seen in the past. Our unique business model allows us to bring you more focused information, giving you more of what you need to know, and less of what you don't.

Packt is a modern, yet unique publishing company, which focuses on producing quality, cutting-edge books for communities of developers, administrators, and newbies alike. For more information, please visit our website: www.PacktPub.com.

PACKT
PUBLISHING

Building powerful and robust websites with
Drupal 6

Build your own professional blog, forum, portal or community
website with Drupal 6.

David Mercer

PACKT

Building Powerful and Robust Websites with Drupal 6

ISBN: 978-1-847192-97-4   Paperback: 362 pages

Build your own professional blog, forum, portal or community website with Drupal 6

1. Set up, configure, and deploy Drupal 6

2. Harness Drupal's world-class Content Management System

3. Design and implement your website's look and feel

4. Easily add exciting and powerful features

5. Promote, manage, and maintain your live website

Elgg Social Networking

Create and manage your own social network site using this free
open-source tool

Mayank Sharma

PACKT

Elgg Social Networking

ISBN: 978-1-847192-80-6   Paperback: 179 pages

Create and manage your own social network site using this free open-source tool

1. Create your own customized community site

2. Manage users, invite friends, start groups and blogs

3. Host content: photos, videos, MP3s, podcasts

4. Manage your Elgg site, protect it from spam

5. Written on Elgg version 0.9

Please check **www.PacktPub.com** for information on our titles

Learning Drupal 6 Module Development

ISBN: 978-1-847194-44-2   Paperback: 310 pages

A practical tutorial for creating your first Drupal 6 modules with PHP

1. Specifically written for Drupal 6 development

2. Program your own Drupal modules

3. No experience of Drupal development required

4. Know Drupal 5? Learn what's new in Drupal 6

5. Integrate AJAX functionality with the jQuery library

6. Packt donates a percentage of every book sold to the Drupal foundation

Drupal 6 Themes

ISBN: 978-1-847195-66-1   Paperback: 291 pages

Create new themes for your Drupal 6 site with clean layout and powerful CSS styling

1. Learn to create new Drupal 6 themes

2. No experience of Drupal theming required

3. Techniques and tools for creating and modifying themess

4. A complete guide to the system's themable elements

Please check **www.PacktPub.com** for information on our titles

2957069